Kick-Start Your Spiritual Growth

Dr. Jeffery Elliott

ISBN: 978-1985318632
ISBN-13: 1985318636

DEDICATION

To all Christians who wish to grow in their faith

CONTENTS

ACKNOWLEDGMENTS

To all the hardworking Christian leaders who have helped me grow in Christ.

Basics for Believers

Purpose: The purpose of this book is to equip believers with the tools and knowledge so they can advance in their spiritual growth and become effective in their service to Christ and His Church.

Format: The format for this book is a set of twelve chapters. Each one is designed to be separate and complete in itself.

Welcome to Kick-Start Your Spiritual Growth! This book has been carefully and prayerfully designed to help you in your walk with Christ. The eleven topics chosen have been selected to build a foundation in three areas of your life:

1. Your daily walk with Christ

2. Your knowledge and study of the Bible

3. The Church and your relationship to it

Each chapter will contain a summary of learning objectives, detailed notes, and a quick review section. Most of the units will have additional scriptures that are not covered in the detailed notes. These references are for a more in-depth study of the topic and should be read as part of your ongoing Bible study as you have time. Make it your goal to read every scripture referenced. Use a highlighter to mark them off as you do.

I have tried to include scripture references every time I mention something the Bible says. They will be in ( ) immediately after each concept. The purpose is for you to examine the scriptures yourself. (See Acts 17:11) Make it your goal to read each of these references. Use a highlighter to mark them off as you read them. Words that are underlined can be found in the dictionary at the end of the book.

Remember, as with anything in life, what you get out of this book will depend on what you put into it. Pray now and every night asking God to help you understand the material, remember it, put it into practice in your own life, and teach it to others.

What Just Happened to You

How shall we escape if we ignore such a great salvation? This salvation, which was first announced by the Lord, was confirmed to us by those who heard him. Hebrews 2:3

In this chapter you will learn:

- ➤ What does it mean to be saved
- ➤ The need for salvation
- ➤ How to be saved
- ➤ How we can be sure we are saved
- ➤ Three important aspects of salvation

Having a good understanding of salvation is important. Causing a believer to doubt or wonder about their salvation is one of Satan's most often used spiritual attacks. You may have already experienced an attack in this area. Knowledge of what God's Word says about your salvation is the key to battling these spiritual attacks.

What Does it Mean to be Saved?

To be saved means that you have come to life. Spiritually, you were dead. It is as though an entire dimension of your life was missing and without it, you walked around like you were in a dark room. Suddenly, the door has been opened to a beautiful, sunny, spring day. Jesus calls this being born again (John 3:3-7). Life will never be the same for you.

To be saved means to be saved from sin. The Bible tells us that Christ <u>redeemed</u> you from sin. To redeem means to buy back. It requires a price and the price paid for you was the death of Jesus Christ.

But what did you do to deserve Jesus dying for you? Nothing! It is by grace you are saved. <u>Grace</u> means receiving something you don't deserve. God's grace is that which comes out of His love; He provided a way to pay for your sins when you didn't deserve it.

When you were born physically, you started out unable to experience all that the physical world offered. You could not walk, talk or eat many of the solid foods that you now enjoy. You had to grow. Even as a child and a teenager there were things that were not within your grasp. You had to mature. The same is true now that you have been born spiritually. You must learn how to talk, walk, eat solid food and get along with others. Some of this requires knowledge, but most of it simply requires practice.

The Need for Salvation

The Bible tells us that God created everything. He has established laws that we are to live by. Unfortunately, we have all broken God's law at some time. This is because we are born with a sin nature, it is in our nature to sin. No one has to teach us how to sin. Our parents did not have to sit down with us and say, "Okay, Johnny, this is how you lie." Many believe that if they try to live a good life that when they die, their good deeds and bad deeds will be compared and as long as their good deeds outweigh their bad deeds, they'll get to go to heaven. But this is not the way it works. If you rob a bank and are brought before the judge, he will not look at how much good you've done in your life and then decide if you should be released. He will judge you for breaking the law and sentence you accordingly. It works the same way in the spiritual world. When you break God's law, you will be judged not on the good deeds you've done, but on the law you've broken and be sentenced accordingly. The Bible tells us the sentence for breaking God's law is death and eternal separation from God in hell. Therefore, our situation is that we stand before God having broken His law and facing the sentence of hell.

The ABC's of Salvation

The Good News is that God loved you so much that he did not want you to be separated from him. So from the very beginning, God had a plan. God sent his only son, Jesus, to earth to live as a man and yet never sin. Jesus died on a cross to pay the death penalty for your sin. Now he wants to save you from that sin and give you eternal life and heaven. To receive this gift from God, all you have to do is Admit, Believe, and Confess.

ADMIT

Admit to God that you are a sinner. Repent, turning away from your sin.

> *... for all have sinned and fall short of the glory of God.*
> Romans 3:23

> *For the wages of sin is death, but the gift of God is eternal life in Christ Jesus our Lord.* Romans 6:23

> *If we claim we are without sin, we deceive ourselves and the truth is not in us. If we confess our sins, he is faithful and just*

and will forgive us our sins and purify us from all unrighteousness. 1 John 1:8-9

It is hard to admit when we've done something wrong. How many times have you gotten into an argument that wouldn't end because you couldn't admit you were wrong even when you knew you were? Pride can easily get in the way of our admitting to God that we are sinners. We must not make the mistake of making excuses for our sin, we must **admit** it. That means to call it what it is, **wrong**!

Admitting Versus Excuse-Making

Admitting:

<u>Example</u>

"Lord, I admit that I used language I shouldn't have. I know it is wrong and ask your forgiveness."

<u>Biblical Example</u>

"But the tax collector stood at a distance. He would not even look up to heaven, but beat his breast and said, 'God, have mercy on me, a sinner.'" Luke 18:13

<u>Can you think of an example? Write it below:</u>

_____

_____

_____

_____

Excuse-Making:

<u>Example</u>

> *"Lord, I know I said that word, but if that person hadn't made me so mad, I wouldn't have said it."*

<u>Biblical Example</u>

> *The man said, "The woman you put here with me – she gave me some fruit from the tree, and I ate it."* Genesis 3:12

Can you think of an example? Write it below:

_____

_____

_____

BELIEVE

Believe that Jesus is God's Son and accept God's gift of forgiveness from sin.

> *God demonstrates his own love for us in this: While we were still sinners, Christ died for us.* Romans 5:8

> *For God so loved the world that he gave his one and only Son, that whoever believes in him shall not perish but have eternal life.* John 3:16

> *Salvation is found in no one else, for there is no other name under heaven given to men by which we must be saved.* Acts 4:12

Jesus answered, "I am the way and the truth and the life. No one comes to the Father except through me. John 14:6

For it is by grace you have been saved, through faith – and this not from yourselves, it is the gift of God – not by works, so that no one can boast. Ephesians 2:8-9

Intellectual Acknowledgement Versus Life-Changing Experience

Knowing about Jesus is not the same as believing in Jesus. It is easy for us to say with our minds that we know Jesus lived and acknowledge the evidence that he was God, but true belief results in a life-changing experience. James wrote, *"You believe there is one God. Good! Even the demons believe that – and shudder."* (James 2:19)

Intellectual Acknowledgement:

An intellectual acknowledgment may cause you to go through the motions; walk down the aisle, be baptized, and join the church. But there seems to be very little change if any in your life. Intellectual acknowledgment will not save you.

Life-Changing Experience:

A true belief in Jesus will result in a change in your life. You can have a true belief in many things. It is a life-changing experience. It causes you to want to live differently.

CONFESS

Confess (say) your faith in Jesus Christ as Savior and Lord.

That if you confess with your mouth, "Jesus is Lord," and believe in your heart that God raised him from the dead, you will be saved. For it is with your heart that you believe and are justified, and it is with your mouth that you confess and are saved. ... for, "Everyone

who calls on the name of the Lord will be saved." Romans 10:9-
10,13

"If anyone is ashamed of me and my words in this adulterous and sinful generation, the Son of Man will be ashamed of him when he comes in his Father's glory with the holy angels." Mark 8:38

Whoever acknowledges me before men, I will also acknowledge him before my Father in heaven. But whoever disowns me before men, I will disown him before my Father in heaven. Matthew 10:32-33

Ways To Confess

➤ Pray to God and tell Him you believe.
➤ Walk down the aisle at the end of any service
➤ Baptism
➤ Tell others about Jesus

Security of Your Salvation

A man walked into a barbershop and asked for a shave. The barber was busy with another customer, so he called for Grace, and a woman walked out from the back and began to shave the customer. The man was amazed at how smooth and well Grace shaved him. He thanked her, paid for the shave and left. The next morning, he noticed that Grace had shaved him so close that he didn't need to shave. As the week progressed, he noticed that he did not need to be shaved. Finally, after a couple of weeks, he went back to the barbershop and asked to speak to Grace. "You shaved me so close I haven't needed to shave for two weeks," he told her. Looking unimpressed she replied, "Once shaved by Grace, always shaved."

It is natural to wonder if you are saved. There are times when we don't feel saved. There will be times in your life when you will sin, and this may cause you to question whether you are saved. However, the Bible makes it clear that our salvation is not based on feelings, but on the completed action of Jesus.

This illustration of the train shows us that our faith must be driven by the fact of what Jesus did, not by our feelings.

The Bible makes it clear that we cannot be good enough to save ourselves. We are saved by grace, not by works (Eph. 2:8-9). If you cannot be good enough to save yourself, then once Jesus saves you, you cannot be bad enough for him to lose you. You are born again when you are saved, and you cannot be unborn. When you are saved, you become a child of God. You are part of the family of God. In a human family, no matter how much a child may mess up, they are still part of that family. It is the same way in God's family.

For I am convinced that neither death nor life, neither angels, nor demons, neither the present nor the future, nor any powers, neither height nor depth, nor anything else in all creation, will be able to separate us from the love of God that is in Christ Jesus our Lord. Romans 8:38-39

I give them eternal life, and they shall never perish; no one can snatch them out of my hand. My Father, who has given them to me, is greater than all; no one can snatch them out of my Father's hand. John 10:28-29

Therefore, if anyone is in Christ, he is a new creation; the old has gone, the new has come! 2 Corinthians 5:17

Three Aspects of Salvation

In Philippians 1:6 Paul writes, *"he who began a good work in you will carry it on to completion until the day of Christ Jesus."* This verse summarizes three aspects of salvation: past, present, and future. The moment you received Christ as your savior, you became a forgiven, freed, child of God. That happened in the past. At that moment, God also gave you some rights and an inheritance. The rights are for you to claim in the present while the inheritance is for you to receive in the future.

The Beginning Point

"He who began a good work in you."

You have been saved. There is a point in your past where you received Christ as your Savior. At that point, you became 'saved.' Jesus told Nicodemus *"no one can see the kingdom of God unless he is born again."* (John 3:3). Thus you have a first birth (physical), and when you are saved, you have a second birth (spiritual). Paul writes, *"Therefore, if anyone is in Christ, he is a new creation; the old has gone, the new has come!"* (2 Corinthians 5:17). At this point, you have the assurance of eternal life and heaven. All of your sins have been wiped out. You have been freed from the penalty of sin. The theological term for this is <u>regeneration</u>.

The Continuing Process

"Will carry it on."

Spiritual maturity is a continuing process you go through. It takes a lifetime. It is the process of the Holy Spirit changing you to be like Christ. It is being freed from the power of sin. This is a process where you work with the Holy Spirit. Paul wrote, ... *continue to work out your salvation with fear and trembling, for it is God who works in you to will and to act according to his good purpose.* (Philippians 2:12-13) The theological term for this is <u>sanctification</u>.

The Final Event

"until the day of Christ Jesus"

Your salvation will one day result in your body being changed into a heavenly body that will experience no pain, hunger, or fatigue. This day will come when Jesus returns for his people. You will also be free from the presence of sin. The theological word for this is glorification.

Listen, I tell you a mystery: We will not all sleep, but we will all be changed – in a flash, in the twinkling of an eye, at the last trumpet. For the trumpet will sound, the dead will be raised imperishable, and we will be changed. For the perishable must clothe itself with the imperishable, and the mortal with the immortality. When the perishable has been clothed with the imperishable, and the mortal with immortality, then the saying that is written will come true: "Death has been swallowed up in victory." 1 Corinthians 15:51-54

Quick Review

➤ The Bible tells us that every one of us needs salvation because we have all sinned (broken God's law). It is easy to receive salvation; you simply have to

    A. Admit you are a sinner.

    B. Believe that Jesus is God's Son and died for your sins.

    C. Confess your faith in Jesus as your Savior and Lord

➤ Once you are saved, you can never lose your salvation. Jesus told us that no one could snatch us from his hand. Paul told us he was convinced that nothing can separate us from the love of God.

➤ There are three important aspects to salvation.

    1. The Beginning Point – Past – regeneration – we were saved and have eternal life and heaven

    2. The Continuing Process – Present – sanctification – we are being changed to be like Christ

    3. The Final Event – Future – glorification – in the future, our bodies will be changed, and we will be free from the presence of sin, death, and the frailties of this body

Important Scriptures on Salvation

Matthew 10:32-33	Don't be ashamed of Jesus
Luke 13:3	You must repent
John 3:16	God loved you so much
John 3:18	Unbelievers stand condemned
John 14:6	Jesus is the only way
Acts 16:31	Believe on Jesus, and you will be saved
Romans 3:23	All have sinned
Romans 5:8	God loved you so much
Romans 6:23	The penalty for sin is death
Romans 10:9-10	Believe in your heart, confess with your mouth
2 Corinthians 6:2	Now is the time
Ephesians 2:8-9	Salvation provided
1 Timothy 2:4	God wants everyone saved
Titus 3:5	We are saved not because of righteous things we've done
James 2:10	Breaking God's law
James 2:19	Don't just think it
2 Peter 3:9	God wants everyone saved
1 John 1:8	Everyone sins
1 John 1:9	Confess your sins

Talking With Our Father

"Lord, teach us to pray, just as John taught his disciples." Luke 11:1

In this chapter you will learn:

- ➤ The Lord's Prayer
- ➤ How to pray in public
- ➤ What to do when others are praying
- ➤ Why prayers go unanswered

Prayer is an important and exciting part of the Christian life. Have you ever thought about what prayer consists of? Many people think of prayer as simply asking for things such as asking God to heal someone or asking God for a new vehicle. While asking is part of prayer, there is much more to prayer.

The Model Prayer
Matthew 6:9-13

Jesus' disciples asked him to teach them to pray. He gave them the example of the Model Prayer better known as the Lord's Prayer. The purpose of the Model Prayer was to be an example, not something that we just repeat word for word. It was intended to show us different aspects of prayer. It can be divided into two main parts: God's concerns and our concerns. God's concerns can be divided into three areas. Our concerns can be divided into three areas. You'll notice that the Model Prayer starts with God's concerns. This means we should be focused more on God's concerns than our own. In fact, when we focus on God's concerns, ours will seem less important and urgent.

God's Name

The Model Prayer starts with "Our Father, who art in heaven, hallowed be thy name." In the Bible, names are very significant. Names were identified with your character. The name Jacob means 'one who deceives' in Hebrew. God changed his name to Israel which means 'one who struggles with God' to indicate a change in his character. The name Naomi means 'pleasant' in Hebrew. She changed her name to 'Mara,' which means 'bitter' in Hebrew because she had lost her husband and both sons.

When the Lord's Prayer says that God's name is to be hallowed, it means that we are to honor or praise God's name. We do this by telling God how great He is. When we have someone, we admire and respect, we tell them so. If you were to meet someone you considered a hero such as a sports star, you might use phrases such as "You were so great in that game. You're the best!" That's how you should be with God. Nobody deserves such praise more than God. In Revelation 4, the Four Living Creatures praise God by saying "Holy, holy, holy is the Lord God Almighty, who was and is, and is to come." (Rev. 4:8) and the 24 Elders praise God by saying "You are worthy, our Lord and God, to receive glory and honor and power, for you created all things, and by your will they were created and have their being." (Rev. 4:11).

Start your prayers with praise to God. For help in learning how to praise God, study the following scripture: Deuteronomy 32; Psalm 8; Psalm 30; Acts 4:24-30.

God's Kingdom

"Your kingdom come." The Kingdom of God can be thought of in two ways. The Kingdom of God is the final kingdom where we will live with God forever. There will be no more imperfect and corrupt human governments. That is in the future, and the Bible tells us we should be praying for that Kingdom to come. But the Kingdom of God can also be seen as the spiritual kingdom of believers. Jesus said, "…the Kingdom of God is within you." (Luke 17:21) To pray, "Thy Kingdom come," is to pray for the advancement of God's Spiritual Kingdom on earth. His Kingdom is expressed in the Church, the body of believers. You can pray for God's Kingdom to come by praying for:

➢ Lost people by name that they would be saved
➢ Your pastor for spiritual growth, protection from the evil one, inspiration, deliverance from temptation.
➢ Missionaries for the message to spread rapidly, to be delivered from evil men.
➢ Other ministers in your church and others.

God's Will

"Your will be done on earth as it is in heaven." In heaven, God's will is done perfectly and without question. It is also done immediately. We can pray for God's will to be done in three areas here on earth:

- Your life
- Your church
- Your community

Once we have our priorities straight by focusing on God's concerns first, we then turn to our concerns.

Our Needs

"Give us today our daily bread." One of our major concerns is our needs. That's why the Lord's Prayer continues with "give us this day our daily bread." Asking for our daily bread doesn't just mean physical bread to eat; it means all our needs for the day. This includes food for our bodies as well as spiritual food for our soul. It also means what is needed that day for our emotional needs. And finally, our financial needs for the day.

By focusing on our needs for today, Jesus is helping us to focus on the present. While we should not ignore the future, too often we get too caught up in the future. Imagine a person who devotes all his life to planning, preparing and providing for the future but fails to live in the present. Then one day, Jesus returns and all the planning, preparing and providing for the future becomes meaningless.

Our Sins

"Forgive us our debts as we also have forgiven our debtors." Although our sins can never cause us to lose our salvation, they can cause us to lose our fellowship with God and others. Just like a child who disobeys their parent; they do not cease to be the child of the parent, but they do lose the closeness and fellowship with the parent. To keep our fellowship with God alive and fresh, we must deal with our sins immediately. We do this in two ways: confessing our sins and asking for forgiveness.

Confessing our sin means 'agreeing with God that it is wrong.' It is easy to confuse this with excuse-making. Excuse-making is when we try to give God reasons why we sinned. "I'm sorry I sinned, but I only did it because of what they did." This is excuse-making. God wants us to simply say (and mean) what we did was wrong. Once we confess it to God then we need to ask his forgiveness. The Bible tells us that God will always forgive us if we confess our sins and ask for forgiveness. (1 John 1:9).

God not only wants us to confess our sins to him, but he wants us to forgive others. Since God always forgives us, we should always forgive others. As you pray, if you are holding something against someone else, take this time to tell God that you forgive them.

Our Protection

"Lead us not into temptation, but deliver us from the evil one." This verse can look unusual to us. "Lead us not into temptation." Does God lead us into temptation? No. The verse simply means that we should ask God to lead us away from temptation. Someone once said, "I can resist anything except temptation." In a way, that is true for all of us. Instead of focusing on resisting temptation, we should ask God to keep us away from temptation. A recovering alcoholic doesn't get better by sitting in a bar and fighting the desire to take a drink. Instead, the recovering alcoholic does best when they stay out of bars and away from temptation. Solomon tells us the best way to avoid adultery is to stay away from the house of the adulteress. (Prov. 5:8).

Did you know you have an enemy that is roaming around this earth trying to destroy you? (1 Peter 5:8) Our only protection from this evil one is God. We need to ask God to deliver us from the evil one every day.

Write out your own prayer in the Model Prayer Format:

_____

_____

_____

_____

_____

Other Aspects of Prayer

Thanksgiving

Another aspect of prayer mentioned in the Bible is thanksgiving. Too often we ask God for something in prayer and then forget to thank him when he answers. Paul tells us to give thanks in all circumstances (1 Thess. 5:18). That means that no matter how bad the situation, you can thank God for something. It has been said, look at God through your problems and he will seem a long way away. But look at your problems through God and you won't see them.

The Psalmist wrote that we should enter His gates with thanksgiving in our hearts (Ps. 100:4) God has done so much for us. He provides everything we need. Jesus died on a cross and paid for all your sins. How many times have you thanked him since you've been saved? Is that enough for all he did? As we enter the church on Sunday morning, we should have thanksgiving in our hearts for all God has done for us.

It is human nature to focus on what we do not have. This leads to grumbling and complaining. When the Israelites complained about how hard life was in the wilderness and about all the things they didn't have, it angered the Lord because they were ungrateful for all the He was doing for them. As a result, fire came and burned some of them up (Num. 11:1). Focusing on what we do not have also causes us to be discontented and we begin to pursue things instead of God. Paul told us to learn to be content in whatever situation we find ourselves (Phil 4:10-13;). By focusing on what God has done for us instead of what we do not have, we will develop a thankful and contented heart. This will, in turn, give us more joy in life.

Persistence

When you pray, don't give up. Keep praying day after day after day. Jesus told his disciples to *pray and not give up* (Luke 18:1). Read

Luke 18:1-8 and Luke 11:5-13. One day in October, a man in his 70's walked into the church where I was the pastor. I had never met him, and this was his first time in our church. At the invitation, he walked down the aisle and received Christ as his Savior. He later shared with me that he had two brothers who were Baptist preachers and a sister who was a devout Christian. All of them had prayed for his salvation for years. His wife and daughter were Christians and had prayed for years as well. None of them ever gave up. After years of persistence, their prayers were answered.

Using A Prayer List

As your prayer life grows, you will find more and more requests to pray for; those who are sick, your government leaders, your pastor, your Sunday School teacher and class, lost friends and relatives and the list can go on and on. It is hard to remember all of these without some list. Some will start a list and find it hard to maintain. After a couple of months, you have a long list with several already answered and crossed off. Then you can find yourself going through page after page with only one or two requests per page. A simple and easy way to maintain a prayer list is by using 3x5 cards for prayer requests. Put one request per card. Keep the cards in a stack or recipe card box. As you pray for a request, move that card to the back of the stack. Some days you may pray for 10 or 12 requests. Other days you may only pray for 2 or 3. But when you pick up your stack to pray the next time, your requests will be ready right where you left off. As requests are answered simply remove the card from your stack. As you need to add requests, make new cards and place them on top of your stack.

How to Pray in Public

When called on to pray in public such as at a worship service, the first rule is to relax. You do not have to use special words or be super spiritual to pray in public. Public prayer is much the same as private prayer. It is just talking to God. Here are some simple guidelines to follow.

➢ Keep your prayer on the subject

Opening Prayers – In an opening prayer, pray for God's presence to be felt in the service. Call upon the Lord to be with us during this service. You can also give thanks for God's provisions and anointing for those who are leading the service.

Offering Prayers – Offering prayers should focus on dedicating the offering to the Lord, thanking him for material provisions, and asking for his blessing on the offering.

Closing Prayers (Benediction)– Closing prayers should include thanking God for his presence during the service. Thanking God for the message. Asking for his blessing on all who are present. Asking for opportunities for all present to share the gospel with others.

Special Prayers – Special prayers are usually for one subject such as local missions, a youth trip, someone who is ill. These prayers should be very specific for the subject. Leave out other items that do not pertain to the reason for the prayer.

➢ Do not bow your head – close your eyes but keep your head up so that it is easier for others to hear you.

➢ Project your voice – As you are praying in public, you are representing the entire congregation to God. If the congregation cannot hear you, they can't participate in your prayer. You don't have to yell, but you should speak as though you are talking with someone across the room.

➢ Take your time – it is all right to have pauses while you think of what to say next. In fact, it adds to your prayer by giving the congregation time to pray silently about what you've just prayed.

➢ Write out your prayer – if you are asked early enough and have time, you may want to write out your prayer. This will give you more confidence and take away some of the fear associated with public speaking. Writing out your prayers is okay. Good Christians have done it for centuries.

What to Do When Others Are Praying

When you are part of group prayer where one person is praying, and everyone else is bowing their heads, you can be an active part of the prayer. By listening to what the person praying is saying and praying along with them or 'agreeing' (Matt. 18:19-20) with them in prayer, you are an active part of the prayer. You can 'agree' with them in prayer by saying (or thinking) 'Yes Lord, I pray this also' or you can offer a silent prayer on the same subject in your own words. Imagine what would happen if every Christian in a worship service was praying for the lost during the invitation instead of thinking about what was for lunch or where they were going after the service. Or what would the offering be like if we all prayed with the usher who was leading the prayer instead of letting our minds wander off?

Why Prayers Go Unanswered

The Bible tells us that God hears our prayers and we know that if he hears our prayers, he will answer. Why then are there times when it seems our prayers go unanswered?

Jesus told us that God loves us like a father loves his children and wants to give us good things (Luke 11:11-13). The first reason our prayer may seem to go unanswered is that God has something better for us, or that God answers our prayer in a way other than what we expected. Since God knows us better than we know ourselves and he also knows our future, we must realize that however he chooses to answer our prayer is best. The three answers we can receive from God are yes, no and wait.

The Psalmist tells us that if we cherish sin (hold on to it, don't confess it, and don't repent of it) in our hearts that God will not listen to our prayers. Isaiah tells us *"Surely the arm of the LORD is not too short to save, nor his ear too dull to hear. But your iniquities have separated you from your God; your sins have hidden his face from you, so that he will not hear."* If it seems God is not listening to your prayers, check your heart for sin. Is there something that you need to confess and repent?

Finally, the key to answered prayer is praying in God's will and abiding in Christ. Jesus told us that if we remain or abide in him we can ask whatever we wish and it will be given to us (John 15:7) We abide in Christ by spending daily time with him praying and reading his Word. We pray in God's will by knowing God's will. We learn what God's will is through his Word.

The Main Thing in Prayer

Do you feel overwhelmed with so much to "do" in prayer? Don't let all this information make you feel like you can't pray because you're afraid you won't do it "right." The main thing about prayer is simply to TALK with God. Don't think you have to do all this every time you pray. Just throw in something new now and then to let your prayer time with God grow instead of becoming stagnant. Think of all this as just more things to talk to God about. Remember, just talk with God.

Quick Review

➢ Prayer is an important part of your new life. Jesus gave us an example of how to prayer called the Lord's Prayer. It shows us to pray for God's concerns first and then our concerns.
➢ Don't forget to include thanksgiving in your prayers.
➢ Pray and don't give up.
➢ Get some 3x5 cards and start a personal prayer list today.
➢ If you pray in public, the first rule to remember is to relax and take your time.
➢ When others are praying, you can be an active part of the prayer by 'agreeing' with the person praying.

For Additional Study

Read *How To Develop A Powerful Prayer Life* by Gregory Frizzell

Read *Return To Holiness* by Gregory Frizzell

Important Scriptures on Prayer

Deuteronomy 4:7	God is near when we pray
1 Chronicles 5:20	God answers prayer when we trust him
2 Chronicles 7:13-14	Prayer changes things (if my people who are called)
Psalm 66:18	Sin blocks your prayers
Proverbs 28:9	Our relationship to God's Word affects our prayers
Matthew 6:5-13	The Lord's Prayer
Matthew 7:7-8	Ask, and you shall receive
Matthew 17:19-21	Have faith when you pray
Matthew 18:19-20	If two agree it will be done
Matthew 21:22	If you believe you will receive
Mark 11:22-26	Believe, and you will receive
Luke 11:1-13	The Lord's Prayer and persistence in prayer
Luke 18:1-8	Keep praying and don't give up
John 14:12-14	Have faith, and it will be done
John 15:7	Remain in Jesus and whatever you ask will be done
John 16:23-24	Ask, and you will receive
Romans 8:26-27	The Holy Spirit helps us when we pray
Ephesians 3:14-21	To Him who is able to do more than we can imagine
Ephesians 6:18	Pray for all the saints

Philippians 4:6-7	Pray about everything
1 Thessalonians 5:17-18	Pray always and give thanks
James 1:6-7	Believe, and you will receive
James 4:2-3	Ask with the right motives
James 5:13-16	The prayer of a righteous man is powerful and effective
1 Peter 4:7	Be self-controlled
1 John 3:21-23	If we obey him we will receive whatever we ask
1 John 5:14-15	If we ask according to his will, he hears us

Dr. Jeffery Elliott

Spending Time With Dad

Very early in the morning, while it was still dark, Jesus got up, left the house and went off to a solitary place, where he prayed. Mark 1:35

In this chapters you will learn:

- ➢ What is a quiet time
- ➢ Why have a quiet time
- ➢ How to have a quiet time

What Is A Quiet Time?

A quiet time is simply time spent with God. It is referred to as a quiet time because God tells us in Psalms "Be still and know that He is God." God told Elijah he was going to pass by the cave. Elijah heard a great wind that tore at the rocks, but God was not in the wind. There was an earthquake, but God wasn't in the earthquake. After the earthquake, there was a fire, but God wasn't in the fire. Then Elijah heard a quiet whisper, and there was God. (1 Kings 19:11-13) Jesus went to a solitary (quiet) place (Mark 1:35). Jesus also

29

told us to go into a closet to pray (Matt. 6:6). The idea is to have no distractions so that you can focus on God and hear him speak to your heart.

Why Have A Quiet Time?

Can you imagine marrying someone you've never met, spoken with or written? Then only getting to see them for one hour one day a week? Having a good relationship under such circumstances would be hard. In fact, your spouse would really be a stranger to you. The same is true about your relationship with God. If you only spend time with God on Sunday Mornings for the worship hour, He is going to seem like a stranger to you. You need time with him every day. You were created to have a relationship with God, and every person who has been effective in service for God has developed the habit of a daily quiet time with God. The fact is you cannot be a healthy growing Christian without it!

A quiet time allows you to

- ➢ give devotion to God
- ➢ get direction from God
- ➢ gain delight in God
- ➢ grow daily like God

A quiet time allows the Holy Spirit to

- ➢ give peace to your heart
- ➢ comfort to your soul
- ➢ bring a time of refreshing

Aspects of A Quiet Time

A quiet time is as personal and individual as you are. What works for one person may not work for another. But there are certain aspects of a quiet time. Some are essential while others are a matter of personal choice.

The Big Three

Every quiet time should include at least three elements. I call these the Big Three: Bible Reading, Prayer, and Quiet (or listening).

Bible Reading

God has given us his Word. It contains everything we need to know about God. But it is not simply a book. It is alive! It is closely connected with his Holy Spirit. Whenever anyone picks up the Bible and reads it, it is not simply the words that enter his brain, but it is also the Holy Spirit that speaks to his heart. Whenever you read God's Word, whether you realize it or not, it is feeding your spirit; it is reaching the depths of your soul. That is why it is important to read the Word of God every day! Imagine feeding your physical body only once a week. How weak would you become? Your spirit needs the nourishment of the Word of God. It is essential to your spiritual growth. Without it, you will remain a spiritual infant.

How should you read the Bible in your quiet time? There are several ways, and as you go through life, you may want to try all of them at different times.

The best way for a new believer is to read the Bible all the way through from beginning to end. There is a reading schedule included at the end of this unit. It lists all the chapters of every book of the Bible. Simply check off the box for each chapter as you read it. Try and read at least one chapter a day. Some chapters are short, and some are long so you may read more than one chapter on some days.

Another way to read your Bible is using a devotional guide and reading the suggested Bible passage. There are hundreds of devotional guides. Some are classics such as *My Utmost for His Highest* by Oswald Chambers, which contains a short scripture and a devotional reading. It has readings for an entire year. Some devotionals are designed for a target group such as women, teens, couples, families, etc. Many Southern Baptist churches provide three devotional magazines which are usually available free of charge. Here are three popular ones produced by Lifeway.

Open Windows is a quarterly general devotional that has for each day a devotional scriptural reading, a devotional thought, a prayer, and a read the Bible through in a year scripture reading.

Stand Firm is a monthly devotional magazine designed specifically for men. It has a devotion for each weekday. The devotionals have a scripture reading and a devotional thought. In addition to the devotions, it also contains articles on current events, spiritual growth, and issues of interest to Christian men.

Journey is a monthly devotional magazine designed specifically for women. It has a devotion for each weekday and one for the weekend. It has a scripture reading and a devotional thought along with a suggested prayer and space for journaling.

Prayer

Prayer is a time for you to communicate with God interactively. Unit 2 covers prayer in detail. A significant portion of your quiet time should be spent in prayer.

Quiet

Have you ever had a conversation with someone who talked so much you couldn't get a word in edgewise? Often we are that way with God. We spend a lot of time talking and then wonder why God doesn't speak to us. That is why our quiet time must have some 'quiet' time; time for us to just listen.

How do we listen to God? First, we have to expect that God will speak to us. Then we have to realize that God can speak to us. This puts us in the right attitude for listening. Then just sit still. Don't be in a hurry. It may take several weeks to get past this point but don't give up, keep at it.

How does God speak to us? God whispers to our hearts. As you practice listening, you will become familiar with his voice. Jesus said, "My sheep know my voice." (John 10:4). As you practice listening to God, you will learn his voice.

Example: God may bring someone to your mind while you are listening. At first, you may think this is just your mind wandering. But in reality, it is God speaking to you. He may tell you to pray for that person or to call them and encourage them. Whatever God tells you to do, you are to do right then.

Options

After you've included the Big Three in your quiet time, you may want to add more. Here are suggestions that some have found meaningful in their quiet times. Remember, these are a matter of personal style.

Music

Music can add a great dimension to your quiet time. It is best to have quiet during your prayer, Bible reading and Quiet, but singing, playing an instrument or even listening to music during some portion of your quiet time can be very uplifting. Billy Graham in his book *Angels* says he feels that singing is reserved as a unique way for humans to praise God because the Bible never mentions angels singing.

Art

Like music, art can add a great dimension to your quiet time. Expressing love or worship for God through art or drawing a picture of scripture are ways of using art in a quiet time.

Journaling

Journaling is the process of putting our thoughts on paper (or computer). It is easy for our thoughts to get mixed up or jumbled when we are going through times of trouble. Putting our thoughts on paper helps us to organize and work through our thoughts. It also gives us an opportunity to record where we are spiritually. As time passes, it can be exciting to look back over a journal and see how God has worked in our lives.

Journals come in many forms. You can purchase a bound book with either lined paper or just blank pages at any bookstore. You can use just a notebook or keep your journal on a computer. It is all a matter of personal choice. Entries in your journal are also a matter of personal choice. You may want to record what you prayed to God and what scripture you read. You may want to write out a memory verse. Recording what God impresses on your heart about a scripture reading that day always makes a good entry. Putting down what is happening to you and how God is leading you through it is another good journal entry. Remember, your journal is for you, and there is no wrong or right way to keep a journal.

How to Have A Quiet Time

Having a daily quiet time is simply a matter of discipline and commitment.

Select a Specific Time

Make your quiet time an appointment with God. Put it on your calendar if necessary. In selecting a specific time, consider starting your day with a quiet time. The various Bible characters all had their quiet time early in the morning. This shows that your time with God is your priority. Whatever time you select, be consistent and meet with God every day at that time.

Choose a Special Place

In choosing a place for your quiet time, remember to keep it simple and distraction free.

Gather the Resources You'll Need

You'll need a few simple resources, to begin with.

- ➤ A Bible
- ➤ A reading guide
- ➤ A notebook
- ➤ A pen or pencil
- ➤ A songbook – if you want to sing.

Begin With the Right Attitudes

The Bible tells us to *"Be still and know that I am God."* (Ps. 46:10), so we should approach our quiet time with an attitude of reverence.

David wrote *"in the morning I lay my requests before you and wait expectantly."* (Ps. 5:3), so we should approach our quiet time with an attitude of expectancy. Expect God to speak to you during your quiet time.

Jesus said, *"Whoever is willing to do what God wants will know..."* (John 17:7)

Follow a Simple Plan

There is no one way to have a quiet time. At times you'll find you need to make changes in your quiet time. But to start off, try to spend 15 minutes with God. Rick Warren, in his C.L.A.S.S. 201, suggests this simple plan to get you started.

1. Relax (1 minute). Be still and quiet. Slow down. Prepare you, heart. Take a few deep breaths and wait on God.

2. Read (4 minutes). Begin reading where you left off the day before. Read until you feel God has told you something.

3. Reflect (3 minutes). Think about what the passage means to your life.

4. Requests (4 minutes). Spend some time talking with God about what He has shown you and pray for requests on your prayer list.

5. Remain (3 minutes). Sit still and quiet and listen to God. Just let him speak to your heart. Ask him and he will.

Make A Commitment

The best time for my quiet time _____

The best place for my quiet time _____

The Bible study/reading plan I will use is _____

The supplies that I want to assemble for my quiet time are:

_____

_____

_____

Quick Review

➤ A quiet time is simply time spent getting to know God.
➤ You need to have a daily quiet time to be a growing, healthy Christian.
➤ The Big Three aspects that should be in every quiet time are
    1. Bible Reading
    2. Prayer
    3. Quiet
➤ To help you start a quiet time, start with 15 minutes a day and
    1. Select a specific time
    2. Choose a special place
    3. Gather the resources you'll need
    4. Begin with the right attitudes
    5. Follow a simple plan

Important Scriptures on Spending Time With God

Genesis 1:27	God created man in his own image
Psalms 16:11	Delight yourself in the Lord
Psalms 29:2	Worship the Lord
Psalms 37:5	Commit everything you do to God
Psalms 46:10	Be still and know that He is God
Psalms 119:18	Seeing wonderful things in God's Word
Proverbs 3:6	Acknowledge God, and He will direct your way
Matthew 4:4	You need more than bread to live
Mark 1:35	Jesus withdrew to a lonely place
Luke 22:39	Jesus withdrew to a lonely place
Luke 5:16	Jesus withdrew to a lonely place
John 4:23	God desires our devotion
John 17:7	Willingness to obey leads to knowledge
Acts 4:13	The effect of being with Jesus
1 Corinthians 1:9	God invites us into a wonderful relationship with his son
2 Corinthians 3:18	You are being transformed into his likeness
Galatians 6:9	Don't give up
Revelation 3:20	Jesus wants to enter our lives and fellowship with us
Revelation 4:11	God deserves our devotion

Bible Reading Record

Old Testament

Genesis

1	2	3	4	5	6	7	8	9	10	11	12	13	14	15	16	17
18	19	20	21	22	23	24	25	26	27	28	29	30	31	32	33	34
35	36	37	38	39	40	41	42	43	44	45	46	47	48	49	50	

Exodus

1	2	3	4	5	6	7	8	9	10	11	12	13	14	15	16	17
18	19	20	21	22	23	24	25	26	27	28	29	30	31	32	33	34
35	36	37	38	39	40											

Leviticus

1	2	3	4	5	6	7	8	9	10	11	12	13	14	15	16	17
18	19	20	21	22	23	24	25	26	27							

Numbers

1	2	3	4	5	6	7	8	9	10	11	12	13	14	15	16	17
18	19	20	21	22	23	24	25	26	27	28	29	30	31	32	33	34
35	36															

Deuteronomy

1	2	3	4	5	6	7	8	9	10	11	12	13	14	15	16	17
18	19	20	21	22	23	24	25	26	27	28	29	30	31	32	33	34

Joshua

1	2	3	4	5	6	7	8	9	10	11	12	13	14	15	16	17
18	19	20	21	22	23	24										

Judges

1	2	3	4	5	6	7	8	9	10	11	12	13	14	15	16	17
18	19	20	21													

Ruth

1	2	3	4

1 Samuel

1	2	3	4	5	6	7	8	9	10	11	12	13	14	15	16	17
18	19	20	21	22	23	24	25	26	27	28	29	30	31			

2 Samuel

1	2	3	4	5	6	7	8	9	10	11	12	13	14	15	16	17
18	19	20	21	22	23	24										

1 Kings

1	2	3	4	5	6	7	8	9	10	11	12	13	14	15	16	17
18	19	20	21	22												

2 Kings

1	2	3	4	5	6	7	8	9	10	11	12	13	14	15	16	17
18	19	20	21	22	23	24	25									

1 Chronicles

1	2	3	4	5	6	7	8	9	10	11	12	13	14	15	16	17
18	19	20	21	22	23	24	25	26	27	28	29					

2 Chronicles

1	2	3	4	5	6	7	8	9	10	11	12	13	14	15	16	17
18	19	20	21	22	23	24	25	26	27	28	29	30	31	32	33	34
35	36															

Ezra

1	2	3	4	5	6	7	8	9	10

Nehemiah

1	2	3	4	5	6	7	8	9	10	11	12	13

Esther

1	2	3	4	5	6	7	8	9	10

Job

1	2	3	4	5	6	7	8	9	10	11	12	13	14	15	16	17
18	19	20	21	22	23	24	25	26	27	28	29	30	31	32	33	34
35	36	37	38	39	40	41	42									

Psalms

1	2	3	4	5	6	7	8	9	10	11	12	13	14	15	16	17
18	19	20	21	22	23	24	25	26	27	28	29	30	31	32	33	34
35	36	37	38	39	40	41	42	43	44	45	46	47	48	49	50	51
52	53	54	55	56	57	58	59	60	61	62	63	64	65	66	67	68
69	70	71	72	73	74	75	76	77	78	79	80	81	82	83	84	85
86	87	88	89	90	91	92	93	94	95	96	97	98	99	100	101	102
103	104	105	106	107	108	109	110	111	112	113	114	115	116	117	118	119
120	121	122	123	124	125	126	127	128	129	130	131	132	133	134	135	136
137	138	139	140	141	142	143	144	145	146	147	148	149	150			

Proverbs

1	2	3	4	5	6	7	8	9	10	11	12	13	14	15	16	17
18	19	20	21	22	23	24	25	26	27	28	29	30	31			

Ecclesiastes

1	2	3	4	5	6	7	8	9	10	11	12

Song of Solomon

1	2	3	4	5	6	7	8

Isaiah

1	2	3	4	5	6	7	8	9	10	11	12	13	14	15	16	17
18	19	20	21	22	23	24	25	26	27	28	29	30	31	32	33	34
35	36	37	38	39	40	41	42	43	44	45	46	47	48	49	50	51
52	53	54	55	56	57	58	59	60	61	62	63	64	65	66		

Jeremiah

1	2	3	4	5	6	7	8	9	10	11	12	13	14	15	16	17
18	19	20	21	22	23	24	25	26	27	28	29	30	31	32	33	34
35	36	37	38	39	40	41	42	43	44	45	46	47	48	49	50	51
52																

Lamentations

1	2	3	4	5

Ezekiel

1	2	3	4	5	6	7	8	9	10	11	12	13	14	15	16	17
18	19	20	21	22	23	24	25	26	27	28	29	30	31	32	33	34
35	36	37	38	39	40	41	42	43	44	45	46	47	48			

Daniel

1	2	3	4	5	6	7	8	9	10	11	12

Hosea

1	2	3	4	5	6	7	8	9	10	11	12	13	14

Joel

1	2	3

Amos

1	2	3	4	5	6	7	8	9

Obadiah

1

Jonah

1	2	3	4

Micah

1	2	3	4	5	6	7

Nahum

1	2	3

Habakkuk

1	2	3

Zephaniah

1	2	3

Haggai

1	2

Zechariah

1	2	3	4	5	6	7	8	9	10	11	12	13	14

Malachi

1	2	3	4

New Testament

Matthew

1	2	3	4	5	6	7	8	9	10	11	12	13	14	15	16	17
18	19	20	21	22	23	24	25	26	27	28						

Mark

1	2	3	4	5	6	7	8	9	10	11	12	13	14	15	16

Luke

1	2	3	4	5	6	7	8	9	10	11	12	13	14	15	16	17
18	19	20	21	22	23	24										

John

1	2	3	4	5	6	7	8	9	10	11	12	13	14	15	16	17
18	19	20	21													

Acts

1	2	3	4	5	6	7	8	9	10	11	12	13	14	15	16	17
18	19	20	21	22	23	24	25	26	27	28						

Romans

1	2	3	4	5	6	7	8	9	10	11	12	13	14	15	16

1 Corinthians

1	2	3	4	5	6	7	8	9	10	11	12	13	14	15	16

2 Corinthians

1	2	3	4	5	6	7	8	9	10	11	12	13

Galatians

1	2	3	4	5	6

Ephesians

1	2	3	4	5	6

Philippians

1	2	3	4

Colossians

1	2	3	4

1 Thessalonians

1	2	3	4	5

2 Thessalonians

1	2	3

1 Timothy

1	2	3	4	5	6

2 Timothy

1	2	3	4

Titus

1	2	3

Philemon

1

Hebrews

1	2	3	4	5	6	7	8	9	10	11	12	13

James

1	2	3	4	5

1 Peter

1	2	3	4	5

2 Peter

1	2	3

1 John

1	2	3	4	5

2 John

1

3 John

1

Jude

1

Revelation

1	2	3	4	5	6	7	8	9	10	11	12	13	14	15	16	17
18	19	20	21	22												

Dr. Jeffery Elliott

The Hardest Step of Obedience

Honor the Lord with your wealth and with the best part of everything your land produces. Then he will fill your barns with grain, and your vats will overflow with the finest wine. Proverbs 3:9-10

In this chapter you will learn:

> The purpose of tithing

> Tithing as an act of worship

> How to tithe

> How to handle the rest of your money

There are three areas of our lives we have trouble turning over to God:

> Our Time

> Our Relationships

> Our Money

The hardest step of obedience seems to be in turning over our money to God. Tithing (giving a tenth back to God) is a step of obedience that pays unbelievable dividends. I can tell you from personal experience that you cannot afford to not tithe.

"I have always tithed," a man told his pastor, "but now I have a problem with tithing. When I began tithing, my weekly income was fifty dollars, and I gave five dollars to the church every Sunday. I was successful in business, and my income rose to five hundred dollars a week, and I gave fifty dollars to the church every Sunday. Now my income is five thousand dollars a week, and I just can't bring myself to give five hundred dollars to my church every week."

"Why don't we pray over it?" the pastor said. He prayed, "Dear God, please make this man's weekly income five hundred dollars a week so that he can tithe."

The Purpose of Tithing

When we hear tithing, we usually think of giving money to the church to support the church, and its ministries. But that is only part of the purpose of tithing. What we do with our money says a lot about our relationship to God. We find four purposes of tithing in Deuteronomy 14:23,29.

> ➤ To teach you to always fear (honor) the Lord
> *The purpose of tithing is to teach you always to fear the Lord your God.*
> ➤ Support the church – the Levites were those who served God as a profession.
> ➤ Feed the poor
> ➤ So the Lord will bless you
>
> *Give it to the Levites, who have no inheritance among you, as well as to the foreigners living among you, the orphans, and the widows in your towns, so they can eat*

and be satisfied. Then the Lord will bless you in all your work.

Part of Worship

Tithing is also part of worship. That is why we have an offering taken during the worship services. In times past, when kings were the norm, if someone wanted to visit a king, they would always bring a gift. The gift you brought showed how much honor you had for the king. God is our king, and as we come before his throne to worship him, we bring our tithes and offerings.

> *No one is allowed to appear before me* (God) *without a gift.* Exodus 34:20

> *Give to the Lord the glory he deserves! Bring your offering and come to worship him.* Psalm 96:8

How to Tithe

How do you tithe? The Bible gives us some guidelines.

➢ Regularly & Proportionately

Paul says you should give each week an amount you have determined. What you give should be based on how much you have earned.

> *You should follow the same procedures I gave to the churches in Galatia. On every Lord's Day, each of you should put aside some amount of money in relation to what you have earned and save it for this offering. I Cor.16:1-2*

➢ Predetermined Amount & Cheerfully

Ten percent is the tithe, but God has blessed some to the extent that they can give above the 10% level on a regular basis. Pray and let God lead you in what percentage He wants you to give.

As you give, it should be something you want to do. Giving simply because you feel it is your duty or you have to do it and in your heart, you would rather not, will not lead to the blessings God has waiting for you.

Each man should give what he has decided in his heart to give, not reluctantly or under compulsion, for God loves a cheerful giver. - 2 Cor. 9:7

Benefits of Tithing

➢ See the power of God

It may seem hard for you to trust God in the area of money. When you begin to trust God, you will see the power of God. If you are never in a position where you need God, you will never see the power of God. But when we place our trust in God, we will begin to see God work in powerful ways in our lives.

"Will a man rob God? Yet you rob me. But you will ask, 'How do we rob you?' In tithes and offerings. You are under a curse – the whole nation of you – because you are robbing me. Bring the whole tithe into the storehouse, that there may be food in my house. Test me in this," says the Lord Almighty, "and see if I will not throw open the floodgates of heaven and pour out so much blessing that you will not have room enough for it."   Malachi 3:8-10

➢ You will be blessed

If you are generous in your giving back to God, God will be generous in giving to you. If you are stingy in giving to God, God will be using that same measure as He gives to you. Of course, you must remember that your giving must be out of a love for God and not a desire to get more. I have done a budget, kept track of my money, and run the numbers, and still, I don't understand how it works out sometimes. But God has provided financially for me more than I can describe. I don't have a large bank account. I have yet to buy a BMW. Yet, God has always provided more money than I need. It is because as a young man, I committed always to give 10% and above.

> *If you give, you will receive. Your gift will return to you in full measure, pressed down, shaken together to make room for more, and running over. Whatever measure you use in giving – large or small – it will be used to measure what is given back to you.* Luke 6:38

➤ Opens up opportunity

As God sees that you are faithful in the tithe, He will open doors of opportunity for you. George Muller was a minister who was determined to do whatever God told him. He began an orphanage in London during a time when orphans lived in the gutters of the streets and ate whatever garbage they could find. He had no money and started the orphanage on nothing but faith. Over the years God provided, and the orphanage grew. As Muller heard about various missionaries, he would give whatever money he had, believing that if he gave it to God that God would provide. Muller died poor, yet millions upon millions passed through his hands simply because God knew He could trust Muller with His money.

> *Unless you are faithful in small matters, you won't be faithful in large ones. If you cheat even a little, you won't be honest with greater responsibilities. And if you are untrustworthy about worldly wealth, who will trust you with the true riches of heaven? And if you are not faithful with other people's money, why should you be trusted with money of your own?* Luke 16:10-12

➤ Teaches you obedience

A young boy had a puppy he loved very much. He fed the puppy, played with the puppy and loved the puppy. One day he bought a leash and collar and put it on the puppy and took him for a walk. The puppy pulled and strained at the leash. He whined and struggled to get loose and go his own way. Finally, wanting to make the puppy happy, the boy unhooked the leash and let the puppy run free. As the boy watched the puppy frolic, to his horror, he watched the puppy run recklessly into a busy street where he was struck by a car. While on the leash the puppy was safe but as he went his way, he wandered unknowingly into danger. Learning to obey God can be the hardest lesson to learn, but it will give you the greatest life you can have and keep you from countless dangers. Tithing is hard to start, but it will teach you obedience to God.

Handling the Rest of Your Money

➤ Don't put your trust in your money - Matt. 6:19-21

Mark Tidd of Webster, New York describes an experience from his college days:

An old man showed up at the back door of the house we were renting. Opening the door a few inches, we saw his eyes were glassy, and his furred face glistened with silver stubble. He clutched a wicker basket holding a few unappealing vegetables. He bid us good morning and offered his produce for sale. We were uneasy enough that we made a quick purchase to alleviate both our pity and our fear.

To our chagrin, he returned the next week, introducing himself as Mr. Roth, the man who lived in the shack down the road. As our fears subsided, we got close enough to realize it wasn't alcohol but cataracts that marbleized his eyes. On subsequent visits, he would shuffle in, wearing two mismatched right shoes, and pull out a harmonica. With glazed eyes set on a future glory, he'd puff out old gospel tunes between conversations about vegetables and religion.

On one visit, he exclaimed, "The Lord is so good! I came out of my shack this morning and found a bag full of shoes and clothing on my porch."

"That's wonderful, Mr. Roth!" we said. "We're happy for you."

"You know what's even more wonderful?" he asked. "Just yesterday I met some people that could really use them."[1]

➤ Make your money work for God - Matt. 25:14-30

God has entrusted you with his wealth, and he expects you to use this wealth wisely. This section of scripture shows us that God does not give us an income just for us to spend it on our pleasures. He gives us an income for us to invest it wisely so that it will grow into more and that we can use the growth to help others (Eph. 4:28) and further the kingdom of God.

➤ Don't worry about it - Matt. 6:25-34

Jesus told a parable (Luke 12:16-21) about a man who thought he had the future under control. He had so much wealth that he had to tear down his barns and build bigger ones just to hold it all. But he died before he had a chance to enjoy any of it. Isn't it amazing how we worry so much about the future when we don't even know if we'll be here tomorrow! And we tend not to trust the one who does know how long we'll be here. David said in the Psalms that he never saw the righteous (God's people) go hungry. Jesus taught extensively about not worrying about what you need but put God and his kingdom first, and he will take

---

[1] Stories from *Fresh Illustrations for Preaching and Teaching : From Leadership Journal*. Baker Books, 1997. Edward K. Rowell editor.

care of all your needs.

➢ Be responsible with it - Luke 16:10-13

➢ Be careful - 1 Timothy 6:6-10

Many people think money is security, but 1 Timothy 6:9 warns that it can be just the opposite. A few years ago, columnist Jim Bishop reported what happened to people who won the state lottery:

Rosa Grayson of Washington won $400 a week for life. She hides in her apartment. For the first time in her life, she has "nerves." Everyone tries to put the touch on her. "People are so mean," she said. "I hope you win the lottery and see what happens to you."

When the McGugarts of New York won the Irish Sweepstakes, they were happy. Pop was a steamfitter. Johnny, twenty-six, loaded crates on docks. Tim was going to night school. Pop split the million with his sons. They all said the money wouldn't change their plans.

A year later, the million wasn't gone; it was bent. The boys weren't speaking to Pop, or to each other. Johnny was chasing expensive racehorses; Tim was catching up with expensive girls. Mom accused Pop of hiding his poke from her. Within two years, all of them were in court for non-payment of income taxes. "It's the Devil's own money," Mom said. Both boys were studying hard to become alcoholics.

All these people hoped and prayed for sudden wealth. All had their prayers answered. All were wrecked on a dollar sign.[2]

---

[2] Stories from *Fresh Illustrations for Preaching and Teaching : From Leadership Journal*. Baker Books, 1997. Edward K. Rowell editor.

Frequently Asked Questions

I Can't Afford to Tithe. What Should I Do?

You should start somewhere. Pray and decide on a percentage you are willing to give out of your love for God. It could be 2% or 3%. Then about every six months, increase the percentage. And remember, as your income increase, your giving is a percentage of your income and should increase as well.

What Is An Offering?

We hear the phrase "tithes and offerings." An offering is a gift above the tithe. The tithe is always given to your church. An offering can be given to your church, a special offering, or a ministry outside your church.

Will Tithing Make Me Rich?

No. The purpose of tithing is not to make you rich but to honor God. However, God says in His Word that if you tithe, He will open the floodgates of heaven and pour out a blessing upon you. He will rebuke the devourer. The devourer is anything that would un-expectantly devour your wealth. He also says He will open the floodgates of heaven. This means material blessings as well as spiritual blessings. But you must remember that your motive for giving to God must come from a love for God and not a desire to get more.

Do I Tithe On The Gross Or The Net?

The Bible tells us we are to honor God out of the first fruits of our labor. For the farmer, the first fruits are the first part of the harvest. As he harvests this first part, the natural desire is to store it up since anything could happen to the rest of the crop before it is gathered. But God says to give it to him first. That means the farmer must trust that God will protect the rest of the yield. We are to give to God before we give to the government. Otherwise, we are putting

Uncle Sam higher than God the Father.

Quick Review

- ➤ Tithing is a difficult but important step in your walk with God.
- ➤ The purpose of tithing is to teach you to honor God with your money.
- ➤ Tithing is part of worship.
- ➤ You should tithe regularly, proportionately, cheerfully, and in a predetermined amount.
- ➤ There are many benefits of tithing.
  - o You will see the power of God in your life.
  - o You will be blessed.
  - o It will open opportunities.
  - o It will teach you obedience to the Lord.
- ➤ As for the rest of your money, remember it too belongs to God. He expects you to put your trust in Him and not the money you have. You should make it work for God (invest it). Don't worry about it, but be responsible and be careful.

Important Scriptures on Money

Exodus 34:20	No one is to appear before me empty-handed
Leviticus 27:30-33	The tithe is holy to the Lord
Deuteronomy 14:22-23	Set aside a tenth (tithe)
Deuteronomy 14:28-29	Tithe to be used to support church and feed poor
Psalm 46:8	Offering is part of worship
Proverbs 3:9-10	Honor God with the first part of your money
Malachi 3:8-12	Will a man rob God? Test me in the tithe
Matthew 6:19-21	Store up treasures in heaven
Matthew 6:25-34	Seek first the kingdom of God, and He

	will provide
Matthew 19:16-30	The Rich Young Man – sell your possessions
Matthew 22:15-22	Give to Caesar what is Caesar's and to God what is God's
Matthew 23:23	Woe to the Pharisees
Matthew 25:14-30	Parable of the Talents – Make your money for God
Mark 6:3044	God can provide for you
Mark 8:1-9	Trust God and He will provide for your needs
Mark 10:17-31	Rich Young Man – Don't let money come between you and God
Mark 12:13-17	Give to Caesar what is Caesar's and to God what is God's
Mark 12:41-44	The widow's offering
Luke 3:10-14	John the Baptist on possessions – if two tunics, give one away
Luke 6:38	The measure you to give, it will be given back to you
Luke 9:10-17	God will feed you
Luke 11:42	Woe to the Pharisees
Luke 12:15-21	Parable of the Rich Fool – Don't trust in your wealth
Luke 12:22-34	Seek first His kingdom
Luke 16:1-15	Parable of the Shrewd Manager – use wealth for others
Luke 18:18-30	Rich Young Man – use wealth for others
Luke 19:11-27	Be responsible with the wealth God has given you

Luke 20:20-25	Give to Caesar what is Caesar's and to God what is God's
Luke 21:1-4	The widow's offering
Acts 5:1-11	Ananias and Sapphira – Don't lie about your offering to God
Romans 12:8	Some are given a spiritual gift of giving more
1 Corinthians 9:1-14	Those who preach should make their living by preaching
1 Corinthians 16:1-2	Give weekly and proportionately
2 Corinthians 8:1-4	They gave beyond their ability
2 Corinthians 9:6-15	Decide before you come to church what you will give
1 Timothy 6:6-10	Beware the love of money
James 4:13-17	Do not boast about what you will do tomorrow

Living Life The Jesus Way

But just as he who called you is holy, so be holy in all you do; for it is written: "Be holy because I am holy" 1 Peter 1:15-16

In this unit you will learn:

- ➤ How to set your desires on Godly things

- ➤ How to set your mind on Godly things

- ➤ What to get rid of in your life

- ➤ What to add to your life

- ➤ And a great principle to live your life by

You are now a new life; a new creation brought about by God. The Bible tells us that when we receive Christ as our Savior, we are born again. Think of your new life as starting all over. If you had your life to live over how would you live it? What would you do differently? God wants your new life to be the best it can be. Since He designed you and created you, only He knows the best way for you to live. God wants you to live a holy and moral life. Of course, that is impossible without the help and constant aid of the Holy Spirit. But it is not all up to the Holy Spirit. We must be willing to work with the Holy Spirit as Paul says, *"...continue to work out your salvation with fear and trembling."* Philippians 2:12

The Bible speaks over and over about living a holy life. Let's look at just one passage of scripture that helps us understand how to live a holy life, Colossians 3:1-25. Read it now.

Setting Your Heart and Mind

Paul tells us to set our hearts on things above. Our hearts represent our desires. So, Paul is telling us that we should desire things above. Begin wanting the things of God. Things like peace that is so great you can't understand it, you just experience it. Desire that the lost will be saved. The desire to be pleasing to God. Desire the return of Jesus. Usually, we think of desires as something that is uncontrollable. Since Paul tells us to 'set our hearts,' then it must be possible for us to control what we desire. Begin by asking God in prayer to give you these desires.

Paul tells us that since we have been raised with Christ that we should set our minds on things above because that is where Christ is. You set your mind on all kinds of things. Setting your mind is thinking on something over and over. As Christmas draws closer, children set their minds on what toys they want. As an important appointment draws near you, set your mind on what will happen. When you get up in the morning, you set your mind on what needs to be done that day. Paul is telling us that just as our minds are filled with things that are happening here on earth, we should deliberately think about things above. What does Jesus want us to do today? Who will God bring along our path that He wants us to share the gospel with? What will it be like when Jesus comes back, and we are raptured? The Bible tells us that our actions come out of our thoughts. If we think sinful thoughts, it will lead us to sinful actions. If we think righteous thoughts, it will lead us to righteous actions.

Put To Death

To help us set our hearts and minds on things above, Paul tells us we must 'put to death' certain things that belong to our earthly nature. Death is a separation. Therefore, if we are to 'put to death' something, it means we are to separate it from us. You must separate these things of the natural self from your new life in Christ.

Death is the absence of life. Something that is dead cannot move, it cannot act, it has no will of its own. 'To put to death' means that you do not give it any action or movement. Do not give action or movement to such things as Paul lists.

Death is an end. 'To put to death' then would mean that it would be the end of something. Paul gives us a list of things that we are to put an end to in our lives.

Sexual Immorality

We are to begin living a holy and moral life by putting to death sexual immorality as the New International Version puts it. The King James Version calls it fornication. The living Bible calls it sexual sin. The word used in the Greek is *porneia,* and it is the root for our word pornography. It means *any biblically unlawful sexual intercourse.* To better understand what is biblically unlawful we must understand God's perspective of sex.

Usually, when we think of sex, we think of physical pleasure. But God created sex to bring about life. Sex was designed for us to participate with God in the creation of a new human being, to give life to another. To bring into existence another soul that will praise and serve God. The physical pleasure side of it was to be an encouragement for us to want to bring about these new lives and for a married couple to share a deep, intimate, exclusive love. This new human being that was given life by sex was to be brought into existence out of love.

Unfortunately, Satan wants to pervert everything that God does. And by perverting sex, he perverts God's plan for humans. Think about it for a minute, every form of sexual sin is done for physical pleasure, not to give life to another human being. Homosexuality will never result in the birth of a baby. Adultery is never done to create a new life. God's plan was for one man to unite with one woman for an entire lifetime, working together, living together, loving together to create new lives and training these new lives to live for God. (Malachi 2:15)

How do you 'put to death' sexual immorality? If you are single, you must not engage in sexual intercourse with anyone. If you are married, you can only have sexual intercourse with your spouse. For more info on what is biblically unlawful see Leviticus 18.

See 1 Corinthians 6:9; 12-20; Ephesians 5:5; Galatians 5:19-21 and Revelation 21:8.

Impurity

Paul continues with impurity. If porneia strictly means sexual intercourse, that leaves open a wide range of sexual activity. Christian youth often ask just how far they can go in the sexual realm before they cross the line into sin. People will always look for a loophole that will allow them to engage in as much sexual activity as possible. That is why Paul did not stop at porneia but added to it akatharsian, impurity or moral uncleanness. This word means immoral sexual conduct. Impurity would include all other sexual acts that porneia leaves out. Paul is making it clear that we must live sexually moral lives.

How do you 'put to death' impurity? If you are single, you must not engage in any sexual activity. If you are married, you must keep all sexual activity between you and your spouse.

Lust

Paul adds to the list pathos. It is often translated as passion or inordinate affection and in Paul's writings is used to denote shameful passion. It gives the idea of a person who is a slave to their passions or emotions. God wants us to rule over our emotions instead of letting our emotions rule over us.

How do you 'put to death' lust? You must learn to say no to passions that become obsessive. Evaluate the decisions you make and ask yourself if you are making this decision based on your emotion or based on God's Word.

See Mark 4:19; 5:28; 1 Corinthians 10:6; Galatians 5:17; Romans 1:24; 6:12.

Evil Desires

Paul then adds epithumia, which means a longing or a desire and puts the adjective kaken, which means evil. The idea is that this is a longing for sin, sinful acts or sinful things not necessarily acted upon. Since Paul put this in the list at this point, he was covering the arena of the mind in areas of sin. It is possible to keep yourself from committing a sinful act and yet still long for it in your heart and mind. This is probably the hardest to control.

How do you 'put to death' evil desires? By replacing them with godly desires. This is done by working on your relationship with Christ Jesus and taking captive every thought. When you begin to desire sinful things, stop; confess to God your evil desire, ask God to change your desires to be godly desires. This is something you must work on constantly.

Greed

Paul concludes this list with greed. It is also translated as covetousness. The Greek word is pleouexia and means an insatiable desire to have more. It is the opposite of the desire to give. Paul writes that this is the same as idolatry. C. F. D. Moule writes "idolatry is an attempt to use God for man's purposes, rather than to give oneself to God's service." Greed is a worshipping of material things instead of worshipping the one true God. It is setting material possessions above God.

How do you 'put to death' greed. By worshipping only God and setting priorities. Set God as your number one priority, family as second, yourself as last. Then ask yourself if your decisions match your priorities. Examine your attitude toward material possessions. Do you put them before God? Would the desire for material possessions cause you to miss church? Or stop you from giving to charity or the church?

See also Romans 1:29; 1 Corinthians 5:10-11; 6:10-11

Rid Yourself of

Paul continues with how to live a holy and moral life by telling us to 'rid yourselves.' The Greek phrase Paul used means to take off clothing. Imagine waking up and discovering yourself wrapped only in a coat that is infested with maggots and covered with sewage. Your first reaction would be to rip the coat off and throw it as far from you as possible. That is what God wants us to do with the following.

Anger

Here Paul is talking about a settled feeling of hatred. It permeates your whole attitude and life.

Rage

Rage is a quick temper. You flare up over the slightest thing and often do it without fully understanding the circumstances. See 2 Corinthians 12:20

Malice

Malice is the deliberate intention to harm. We can do it without even realizing we are. It is often found in marital arguments. We know how to use words to hurt our spouse deliberately. It is also found in all other aspects of life.

Slander

Slander is the defamation of human character. It is the vilifying of a person by lies and gossip. See Titus 3:2

Filthy Language

This means both obscene speech and abusive language.

Lying

Lying is pretty self-explanatory, but an area that we may not realize we lie would be untrustworthy promises and pledges. Promising to do something and not following through is the same as lying.

Clothe Yourself with

Since you have thrown off that maggot infested, sewage covered coat, you need to put on some new, clean clothing. Because we still deal with the old nature, it is hard for us to put to death and rid ourselves of the things Paul lists. That is why we need the work of the Holy Spirit every day in our lives. As we spend time with God, the Holy Spirit transforms us into the likeness of Christ. Without the work of the Holy Spirit, we cannot accomplish the putting to death and the ridding ourselves. Paul tells us to put on the following.

Compassion

Another word would be mercy. It is a heartfelt longing to help the less fortunate. It is compassion that created hospitals, orphanages, and homeless shelters. It means to feel sympathy for another.

Kindness

A good definition of kindness is 'the man whose neighbor's good is as dear to him as his own.' It is seeking to do good to others.

Humility

Humility is when we recognize that God is the creator and we are the created. Since God created us, everyone is equal. One person is not better than another person. There is no room for arrogance.

Gentleness

Gentleness means consideration for others. It is a willingness to waive one's rights.

Patience

Patience means to endure wrong. It puts up with the exasperating conduct of others rather than fly into a rage or despair.

Bear with One Another

Bearing with one another means to overlook others shortcomings realizing that none of us are perfect and others have to put up with us at times. Bear is the root word for support, as a post would bear a weight, we should support our fellow Christians as they struggle with their burdens.

Forgive

The forgiveness that the Bible speaks of means a gracious pardon. Forgiving without having to remind the person of their offense.

Love

The Greek word is agape, and it means wanting the best for the other person. Agape is a verb and denotes action, not a feeling. See 1 Corinthians 13:4-8

Do All in the Name of the Lord Jesus

Paul concludes this section by giving us an overall principle by which we are to live, our words and actions should reflect what Christ himself would say and do.

Quick Review

- ➤ You can choose your desires and thoughts.
- ➤ Separate yourself from
  - o sexual immorality
  - o sexual impurity
  - o lust
  - o evil desires
  - o greed
- ➤ Throw away from you
  - o Anger
  - o Rage
  - o Malice
  - o Slander
  - o filthy language
  - o lying.
- ➤ Add to your life
  - o Compassion
  - o Kindness
  - o Humility
  - o Gentleness
  - o Patience
  - o bearing with one another
  - o forgiveness
  - o love.
- ➤ All your words and actions should reflect what Jesus would say and do.

Important Scriptures on Living a Moral and Holy Life

Matthew 5:1-7:29	The Sermon on the Mount
Romans 1:18-32	God gave the sinful over to a depraved mind
Romans 8:1-17	The two natures
Romans 12:1-2	Be transformed by the renewing of your mind
Romans 12:9-21	How you should live
1 Corinthians 6:9-20	Feel from sexual immorality
1 Corinthians 7	Marriage
1 Corinthians 10:6-13	God will provide a way out of temptation
2 Corinthians 6:14-7:1	Purify yourself
Galatians 5:19-24	Crucify the sinful nature
Galatians 6:7-8	Reaping what you sow
Ephesians 4:17-5:21	Living as children of light
Philippians 4:8-9	Think on these things
1 Thessalonians 4:1-8	Be holy and live a holy life
Hebrews 12:1	Throw off everything that hinders
James 4:7-10	Resist the devil
1 Peter 1:13-16	Be holy
1 Peter 2:11-12	Abstain from sinful desires
1 Peter 4:3-4,7	Do not live like this
2 Peter 1:5-9	Make every effort to add to your faith…
2 Peter 3:11-14	How should we live?
Revelation 21:8	The immoral will burn in hell
Revelation 22:15	The immoral will be outside of heaven

Living Life Out Loud

You will be my witnesses in Jerusalem, and in all Judea and Samaria, and to the ends of the earth. Acts 1:8

In this chapter you will learn:

➤ The importance of witnessing

➤ Developing and sharing your testimony

➤ A simple plan for sharing the Gospel

You Are The Light of The World

St. Francis Assisi once said, "Preach the Gospel always, use words if necessary." Jesus said that we are the light of the world (Matt. 5:14). We should live our lives in such a way that people see God in us. But, there are times when we need to use words. Paul wrote, "no one seeks God." (Rom. 3:11) We do not seek out God on our own. God is the one who comes looking for us. Jesus told the parable of the shepherd who had 99 sheep and one that was lost (Luke 15:3-6). The shepherd went in search of the one lost sheep. God goes in search of lost people. When a lost person shows interest in God by going to church or asking questions, it is really God calling that person. It is the Holy Spirit working on their heart. And God will use you to reach these people. God will put you in their path at the right moment for you to be a witness to them. It is called a divine appointment and is one of the most exciting moments in the life of a Christian. You will have two choices at this moment. You can live out loud and be used by God, or you can simply keep quiet and miss out on the single most exciting event in your life; being used by God. And when you speak up, remember, you don't do this alone, the Holy Spirit is working in the person's heart even though it may seem like your words are having no effect.

Telling What Happened to You

Billy Sunday, the great evangelist of the early twentieth century was told right after his conversion that he should develop a daily habit of spending 15 minutes in prayer, 15 minutes reading his Bible, and 15 minutes telling someone about Jesus. He attributed his evangelistic success to these three daily habits. Talking to others about God is very simple. You don't have to know any more than you already know. All God is asking you to do is be a witness of your encounter with God. You don't have to know all the answers to their questions, simply tell them what God did in your life. To help you, there is a simple format that has been effectively used by thousands of Christians. Tell about your life before you were saved, say you had a life-changing experience, and tell of the recent benefits of having Christ in your life. When you're speaking to someone who is lost, try not to use 'churchy' words. Instead, try to use everyday language so they can understand.

It is important to write out your testimony and learn it so it is second nature to you and you can share it with someone without sounding mechanical. When you share it, you don't have to say it word for word as you wrote it. Use your written testimony as a guide.

It is important to move into it naturally. As you're talking with someone, look for opportunities to move into your testimony. For example, someone may be talking about a fear of dying and your testimony may include your own feelings of fear of death. You could say, "I know what you mean. There was a time in my life when I was in constant fear of death." And then proceed with the rest of your testimony.

Life Before Christ

What was your life like before you got saved? Did you live in fear and worry? Was your life wrecked by sin? Were you quietly going along with life? Feelings of loneliness, guilt, lack of purpose may have been part of life without Christ.

Maybe you were saved at a young age and did not experience much of life without Christ. In this case, your pre-conversion experience would be very short. You could start out with "I'm glad I know I have the forgiveness of God and the assurance I will go to heaven."

This does not need to be a lengthy background of your life. It should only be about one minute; otherwise, you may lose their attention. Take some time to write down some ideas of what life was like before you got saved. Think about those things that caused you to be receptive to the Gospel.

_____

_____

_____

_____

_____

What God Used to Begin to Open My Eyes

What was it that God used to get your attention? Was it a book you read, a person who talked with you about God or some event in your life? Briefly tell what brought you to the point of salvation.

This section of your testimony should not exceed one minute. Take some time to write down some ideas.

_____
_____
_____
_____
_____

Life Changing-Experience

The purpose of your testimony is to create a desire in the person to want to know how to go to heaven. At this point you do not want to tell them how you accepted Jesus. You merely want to 'wet their appetite'. So, at this point you simply say,

"I had a life-changing experience."

How Christ Has Affected My Life

Next, tell some of the recent benefits of having Christ in your life. Remember to focus on events that reflect God's faithfulness to you. Also, share evidence of your assurance of heaven. Close with a statement of assurance such as "I know that if I were to die tonight, I would spend eternity in heaven."

This section of your testimony should not exceed one minute. Take some time to write down some ideas.

_____
_____
_____
_____
_____

The Key Question

After sharing your testimony, it is important to move from your salvation to their salvation. The best way to do this is by asking the following question.

"Let me ask you a question. In your personal opinion, what do you understand it takes for a person to go to heaven?"

Their answer will fall into one of the following categories of answers

> ➢ Faith – the way to heaven is by believing on Jesus

> ➢ Works – the way to heaven is by being a good person, trying hard, good deeds

> ➢ Unclear – their answer isn't clear enough to put in one of the previous categories

> ➢ No Opinion – I don't know how to get to heaven

If their answer is unclear, ask some questions such as "Do you mean by being good enough you get to heaven?" If their answer is a works or no opinion answer, ask them if you can share with them how the Bible answers that question. If they say yes, move on to the plan of salvation. If they say no, then realize that you have completed what God wanted you to do and wait for another opportunity at another time.

A Simple Plan

There are several valid plans for presenting the Gospel. The following is a simple, easy to learn and remember plan. It is called the ABC's of salvation. Under each letter, there are one or two verses to support the point. It is important to memorize the verses for each letter and use them in your presentation.

ADMIT

Admit to God that you are a sinner. Repent, turning away from your sin.

... for all have sinned and fall short of the glory of God. Romans 3:23

For the wages of sin is death, but the gift of God is eternal life in Christ Jesus our Lord. Romans 6:23

BELIEVE

Believe that Jesus is God's Son and accept God's gift of forgiveness from sin.

For God so loved the world that he gave his one and only Son, that whoever believes in him shall not perish but have eternal life. John 3:16

CONFESS

Confess your faith in Jesus Christ as Savior and Lord.

That if you confess with your mouth, "Jesus is Lord," and believe in your heart that God raised him from the dead, you will be saved. For it is with your heart that you believe and are justified, and it is with your mouth that you confess and are saved. ... for, "Everyone who calls on the name of the Lord will be saved." Romans 10:9-10,13

The Prayer

At this point, you need to ask them if they would like to receive Christ as their Savior and have the assurance of going to heaven when they die. If they say yes, then lead them in the following prayer.

Dear God, I know I have sinned and that my sin separates me from you. I am sorry for my sin. I believe Jesus died on the cross for me so my sin can be forgiven. God, please forgive me. I ask Jesus to come into my life and be my Savior and Lord. Thank you for saving me. In Jesus Name, Amen.

Follow-up

Once they have prayed to receive Christ, it is not over. It's just beginning. You need to get them into church, into Sunday School and prayer and the Bible. Make sure you have their name and phone number so you can call them. Begin praying for them every day. If they don't have a Bible, get them one. Churches usually have Bibles that are to be given to anyone who needs one. Get them a copy of this book to help them grow as a new believer. Invite them to church and offer to either meet them at church or give them a ride. Make sure they know the times and directions. Finally, talk with the pastor about this new believer.

Quick Review

➤ You are the light of the world.

➤ God wants to use you to reach lost people. He will set up divine appointments with people he has been calling.

➤ You should be prepared by writing out and learning your testimony and learning a simple plan for presenting the Gospel.

➤ The ABC plan is a simple plan that is easy to remember and use.
   o Admit
   o Believe
   o Confess

➤ Be sure to get them into church, Sunday School, prayer and the Bible. Get them a copy of this book.

Important Scriptures on Witnessing

Psalm 96:3,10	Witness to all nations
Ezekiel 3:18-21	Warn those who are perishing
Matthew 4:18-20	I will make you fishers of men
Matthew 28:19-20	Go make disciples
Mark 13:9-12	The Holy Spirit will speak through you
Mark 16:15	Go into all the world and preach the good news
Luke 21:13-15	Don't worry about what to say, I will give you the words
Luke 24:48	You are witnesses
Acts 1:8	You will receive power from the Holy Spirit and be my witnesses
Acts 8:4	They preached the word wherever they went
1 Peter 3:15-16	Be prepared to give an answer
Revelation 12:11	They overcame him by the blood and by their testimony

The Fascinating Story of Israel

The Lord had said to Abram ... "I will make you into a great nation and I will bless you ... and all peoples on earth will be blessed through you." Genesis 12:1-3

In this chapter you will learn:

➤ An overview of the rise of the nation of Israel

➤ Major events in the history of Israel in the Old Testament period

➤ Major events in the history of Israel between the testaments period

➤ Major events in the history of Israel in the Post-New Testament period

➤ Major covenants between God and Israel

An Overview of The Rise of The Nation of Israel in Old Testament Times

Israel is a unique nation with a fascinating story. It is a nation started by God. Throughout the history of Israel, certain events are referred to over and over in scripture because of their impact on Israel.

Abraham

God called Abram to be obedient to him and leave his family and homeland. As Abram was obedient to God, God blessed him and began the nation of Israel through Abram. God changed Abram's name to Abraham. The purpose of this nation was to bring into the world, the Son of God, Jesus Christ.

The Egyptian Slavery and God's Rescue

Initially, Israel went to Egypt to escape a famine and stayed to farm and flourish. The Egyptians became frightened of the rapid growth of the Israelites and decided to enslave them to keep them under control. This period of slavery lasted for 400 years. God heard the cry of his people and raised up a deliverer named Moses. Moses was to lead them back to the land promised to Abraham by God. Because of the disobedience of the Israelites, they were to remain wandering in the wilderness for 40 years (time for the disobedient generation to die off) before they were allowed to enter the promised land.

The Time of the Judges

After 40 years in the wilderness, Joshua led the Israelites into the Promised Land. There they lived as a loose connection of the twelve tribes. During this time, God would raise up Judges or leaders who led a portion of the tribes for a period of time. The last Judge was Samuel, who was unique in that he led all of Israel.

The Unified Kingdom

After a time of living as twelve separate tribes without a common ruler, Israel asked God for a king. God gave them a king and they became a unified kingdom. This unified kingdom only lasted for three kings; Saul, David, and Solomon.

The Divided Kingdom

Because of Solomon's disobedience of worshipping idols brought to Israel by his wives, God split the kingdom into the Northern Kingdom, known as Israel, and the Southern Kingdom, known as Judah. This divided kingdom lasted until the time of the Assyrian conquest.

The Assyrian Conquest

The Northern Kingdom, Israel, never followed God but instead worshipped idols. After repeated warnings, God brought the Assyrian kingdom in to conquer Israel.

The Babylonian Captivity

Judah went back and forth from worshipping God to worshipping idols. After repeated warnings, God brought in the Babylonians to conquer Judah and carry them off to Babylon.

The Return to Israel

After years in exile, God brought his people back to Israel. However, they never again enjoyed the full freedom of ruling themselves and were always under the control of an outside nation. Not until 1948 were the Jews to have their own nation.

An Overview of The Nation of Israel in Inter-Testament Times

Israel was not content being ruled by other nations. At one point, a Syrian Emissary attempts to sacrifice a pig on the altar in the temple to a pagan god. Pigs were considered unclean, and this was a great offense to the Jews. The High Priest, Mattathias was ordered to offer the sacrifice. When he refused, a lower priest agreed to do it. Mattathias was so outraged that he took a spear and killed both the lower priest and the Syrian Emissary and then fled to the hills. He soon died and his grandson Judas took up the command of the rebels who had gathered themselves around Mattathias. Judas was called Maccabeus (the Hammer) because of his guerrilla warfare. This is known as the Maccabean period and is recorded in the Apocrypha in First and Second Maccabeus. They were eventually defeated, and Israel once again was brought under control and became a Roman Province. During this time, the Old Testament was translated from Hebrew to Greek. This translation is still used today in translating from Hebrew to English.

An Overview of The Nation of Israel in New Testament Times

Still, there was unrest in Israel. Even during the time of Jesus, there were revolts and uprisings. Finally, another Judas wannabe rose up and led a revolt. This led to the destruction of Jerusalem in A.D. 70 by Titus, a Roman general and the end of Israel as a nation. From that point until 1948, the Jews were dispersed and persecuted, a people with a country.

The following chart shows the major events in the history of Israel and compares them with other world events around the same period.

The History of Israel in the Old Testament Period

Found In The Bible	Approximate Date	Person, Place or Event	Other World Events
Genesis	2091 B.C.	Abraham	Earliest cuneiform writing (3000 BC). Middle Bronze Age. Pyramids built in Egypt and ziggurats built in Mesopotamia (3000-2000 BC)
"	2066 B.C.	Isaac	Minoan Crete, palace at Knossos, legend of the Minotaur. Indoor bathroom plumbing developed.
"	2006 B.C.	Jacob (Israel) Mother — Son Leah — Reuben Simeon Levi Judah Issachar	King Hammurabi of Babylon writes "code of law." Babylonians develop the 60-minute hour. After Hammurabi's death, Hittites plunder Babylon.

		Zebulun	Assyria rises in strength.
	Bilhah	Dan	
		Naphtali	
	Zilpah	Gad	
		Asher	
	Rachel	Joseph	
		Benjamin	
"	1876 B.C.	Egyptian Slavery	
Exodus	1526 B.C.	Moses – birth	Stonehenge erected in Britain. Late Bronze Age. Mycenaean civilization in Greece. Minoan Crete destroyed by volcano and earthquakes.
"	1446 B.C.	Exodus from Egypt	
Exodus Leviticus Numbers Deuteronomy	1446 - 1406 B.C.	Forty years in the Wilderness	
Joshua Judges	1406 - 1043 B.C.	Period of the Judges	Egyptian pharaoh Ikhnaton develops a monotheistic religion. Tutankhamen becomes pharaoh of Egypt, and reinstates earlier gods.
1 Samuel	1100 – 1050 B.C.	Rise of Samuel (Last of the Judges)	
	1043 – 931 B.C.	Unified Kingdom Kings	

1 Samuel	1043 B.C.	Saul	Trojan horse to defeat Troy. Iron Age. Phoenicians develop an alphabet that is the basis of the modern English alphabet.
2 Samuel	1011 B.C.	David	Etruscans arrive in Italy
1 Kings 1 Chronicles	971 B.C.	Solomon	
"	931 - 586 B.C. 931 – 722 B.C 931 – 586 B.C	Divided Kingdom Northern – Israel – 10 Tribes Southern – Judah – Judah & Benjamin	Greeks colonize Italy and Sicily. First Olympic Games. Founding of Rome (753 BC).
2 Kings	722 B.C.	Assyrian Conquest	
2 Kings	586 B.C.	Babylonian Conquest	Babylon's Hanging Gardens is one of the wonders of the world. Rise of Confucius in China. Rise Buddha in India.
Ezra	538 B.C.	Return from Exile – Rebuilding the Temple	

"	458 B.C.	Return from Exile – Establish Civil Government	Parthenon built. Socrates. Runner carries news of Greek victory at battle of Marathon 26 miles to Athens. Origin of athletic "marathon."
Nehemiah	444 B.C.	Return from Exile – Rebuilding the Wall	

The History of Israel in the Inter-Testamental Period

	336 B.C.	Beginning of the Hellenistic Period	Alexander the Great conquers the known world. Time of Plato and Aristotle. Hippocratic oath written.
	312 – 63 B.C.	Ptolemy & Seleucid Rule	Great Wall of China built. Mayan calendar invented. First Roman gladiator games.
	285 – 247 B.C.	Septuagint – O.T. translated into Greek	
1 Maccabees	167 B.C.	Antiochus IV sets up statue of Zeus in Temple Mattathias slays Syrian Emissary Judas called Maccabeus (The Hammer) assumes	

		command of the revolt	
	63 B.C.	Judea becomes a Roman Province	Cleopatra, last Egyptian queen, rules. Julius Caesar defeats Egypt.

The History of Israel in the New Testament & Post New Testament

Wars of the Jews - Josephus	A.D. 70	Destruction of Jerusalem and Herod's Temple End of Israel as a nation
	A.D. 70 - 1947	Jewish Dispersion and Persecution
	A.D. 1948	Establishment of new Israelite nation

Dr. Jeffery Elliott

Our Father's Book

All scripture is God-breathed and is useful for teaching, rebuking, correcting and training in righteousness, so that the man of God may be thoroughly equipped for every good work. 2 Timothy 3:16-17

In this chapter you will learn:

- ➢ How the Bible is arranged and why
- ➢ How the Bible was written
- ➢ What authority the Bible has in your life
- ➢ How to get the Bible into your life
- ➢ How to study the Bible
- ➢ How to do Christian Meditation

How The Bible Is Arranged and Why

The Bible is 66 different books. We have combined these books into one cover for convenience. It took 40 people over 4,000 years to complete these 66 different books. They were written using three different languages and on three different continents. As you read through the Bible, it can seem like the books are arranged almost randomly, but there is an order to the books. The following chart shows how the books of the Bible are arranged.

Old Testament	New Testament
The Law	**Gospels**
Genesis	Matthew
Exodus	Mark
Leviticus	Luke
Numbers	John
Deuteronomy	
	History
History	Acts
Joshua	
Judges	**Paul's Letters**
Ruth	Romans
1 Samuel	1 Corinthians
2 Samuel	2 Corinthians
1 Kings	Galatians
2 Kings	Ephesians
1 Chronicles	Philippians
2 Chronicles	Colossians
Ezra	1 Thessalonians
Nehemiah	2 Thessalonians
Esther	
	General Letters
Poetry	Hebrews
Job	James
Psalms	1 Peter
Proverbs	2 Peter
Ecclesiastes	1 John
Song of Solomon	2 John
	3 John

Major Prophets	Jude
Isaiah	Revelation
Jeremiah	
Lamentations	
Ezekiel	
Daniel	
Minor Prophets	
Hosea	
Joel	
Amos	
Obadiah	
Jonah	
Micah	
Nahum	
Habakkuk	
Zephaniah	
Haggai	
Zechariah	
Malachi	

The Inspiration and Authority of The Bible

The Bible is not like any other book. It is not a science book, a novel, or a rule book. The Bible is God's revelation of himself to mankind. The Bible is so closely connected with God that you cannot read it without being in the presence of God. It is like a living book because when you read it, it is not your mind that is taking in the information, it is the Holy Spirit of God that is whispering it to your soul. It brings nourishment, refreshment, and guidance to our soul in ways we cannot understand. Without it, our soul suffers.

But how did God get his revelation to man? The first five books of the Old Testament are known as the Law and were written down by Moses. In the case of these first five books, God literally spoke them to Moses, and he wrote down what God said.

Then the Lord said to Moses, "Write down these words" Exodus 34:27

As for the writings of the prophets, God used visions, dreams and the whispering of the Holy Spirit to their hearts. And for the New Testament, God spoke through his Son, Jesus Christ and the whisperings of the Holy Spirit to the Apostles.

In the past God spoke to our forefathers through the prophets at many times and in various ways, but in these last days he has spoken to us by his Son. Hebrews 1:1-2

Then the Lord reached out his hand and touched my mouth and said to me, "Now, I have put my words in your mouth." Jeremiah 1:9

Above all, you must understand that no prophecy of Scripture came about by the prophet's own interpretation. For prophecy never had its origin in the will of man, but men spoke from God as they were carried along by the Holy Spirit. 2 Peter 1:20-21

All Scripture is God-breathed and is useful for teaching, rebuking, correcting and training in righteousness. 2 Timothy 3:16

Because God is the creator of all things, he is the owner of all things. He has the final word. Therefore, his word is the final authority in all things. And because God is Creator, he knows best how life works. He gave us his Word that we might live life in the best way. If God's Word tells us to do something, yet our feelings and desires tell us to do something else, God's Word has authority over our feelings and desires and should be obeyed. God's Word is also above man's law. We are to obey man's law except where it conflicts with God's Word. If man passes a law that says we are not to worship the one true God, we must not obey that law but instead obey God's Word that says "You shall have no other gods before me." (Exodus 20:3)

Getting A Grip on Your Bible

If you were to hold your Bible with only your little pinky, it would be easy for someone to snatch it from your hand. But if you grabbed it with all your fingers, you could hold onto it tightly. This is an illustration of how we are to use the Word of God.

Hearing

Hearing the Bible is an important way of getting God's Word into your life. You hear it through a Bible-based sermon, audio Bibles, or a discussion of the Bible in Sunday School or on the radio. Hearing the Bible is like holding it with your pinky. You need to hear it, but you need more.

To improve your hearing, you need to:

- Be ready and eager to hear God
- Deal with attitudes that prevent hearing God
    - A closed mind: is fear, pride or bitterness preventing me from hearing God?
    - A superficial mind: am I serious about wanting to hear God speak?
    - A preoccupied mind: am I too busy and concerned with other things to concentrate on what God has to say?
- Confess any sin in your life
- Take notes on what you hear
- Act on what you hear

Reading

Reading the Bible will get more of it into your life. You should read it using some logical plan. Read it in a relaxed environment so you can concentrate on what you are reading. Reading is like holding the Bible by your ring finger. Combined with hearing, it gives you a greater grip on your Bible. But you need more.

In reading your Bible, you should:

➤ Read it systematically
➤ Use a Bible without notes
➤ Read it in different translations
➤ Read it aloud quietly to yourself
➤ Choose a reading plan and stick with it

Studying

Studying the Bible involves more than just reading. It takes time. It requires you to dig a little deeper. The secret of effective Bible study is knowing how to ask the right questions: who, what, when, where, why, and how. Ask these questions and use some study tools to help you answer them. Think of studying as the middle finger of your grip on the Bible.

Here is a list of some of the tools you can easily find and purchase.

➤ Different Translations
➤ Study Bible
➤ Concordance – should match the translation you use the most
➤ Bible Handbook – Halley's Bible Handbook considered the best
➤ Commentary – The international Bible Commentary by F.F. Bruce or Matthews Bible Commentary
➤ Bible Atlas – Macmillan or Moody considered the best
➤ Word Study
➤ Pictorial Bible Dictionary
➤ Bible Encyclopedia

Memorizing

Memorizing gets the Word of God inside you as nothing else can. Think of memorizing as the index finger of your grip on the Bible.

Memorizing is important because it

➤ Helps you resist temptation – *I have hidden your Word in my heart that I might not sin against you.* Ps 119:11

➤ Helps you make wise decisions – *Your Word is a lamp to guide me and a light for my path.* Ps 119:105

➤ Strengthens you when you're under stress – *Your promises to me are my hope. They give me strength in all my troubles; how they refresh and revive me!* Ps 119:49

➤ Comforts you when you're sad – *Your words are what sustain me … they bring joy to my sorrowing heart and delight me.* Jer. 15:16

➤ Helps you witness to unbelievers – *Always be prepared to give an answer to everyone who asks you to give the reason for the hope that you have.* 1 Peter 3:15

Three keys to memorizing are repetition, repetition, repetition.

Twelve Tips on Memorizing

1. Pick a verse that speaks to you.
2. Say the reference before and after the verse.
3. Read the verse aloud many times. Record it!
4. Break the verse into natural phrases.
5. Emphasize key words when quoting the verse.
6. Write down the verse and erase a word at a time.
7. Write out the verse on a flash card.
8. Carry some cards with you at all times for review.
9. Display your verses in prominent places.
10. Always memorize the verse word-perfect.
11. Put the verse to music. Write a song!
12. Get a partner so you can check each other.

At the end of this chapter there is a Scripture Memory Course to help you get started. Begin with the first verse and work on it for a week or two. Then move on to the next verse while reviewing the previous verse.

Meditating

Today we often think of meditation as sitting in the lotus position and chanting some phrase over and over. Zen meditation taught in America today teaches people to empty their minds. Meditating on God's Word is completely the opposite. When you meditate on God's Word, you fill your mind with God's Word! You think on it over and over to discover how you can apply its truth to your life. The Bible tells us to *"be transformed by the renewing of your mind"* (Rom. 12:2) and to *"set your mind on things above"* (Col. 3:2). Think of meditating as the thumb of your grip on the Bible.

Six Ways to Meditate on a Verse

1. Picture it! Visualize the scene in your mind.
2. Pronounce it! Say the verse aloud, each time emphasizing a different word.
3. Paraphrase it! Rewrite the verse in your own words.
4. Personalize it! Replace the pronouns or people in the verse with your own name.
5. Pray it! Turn the verse into a prayer and say it back to God.
6. Probe it! Ask the following nine questions: Is there any ...
   - Sin to confess?
   - Promise to claim?
   - Attitude to change?
   - Command to obey?
   - Example to follow?
   - Prayer to pray?
   - Error to avoid?
   - Truth to believe?
   - Something to thank God for?

Applying

All the knowledge of God's Word will do nothing if you do not apply it to your life. To apply God's Word to your life you need to ask three questions:

1. What did it mean to the original hearers?
2. What is the underlying timeless principle?
3. Where or how could I practice that principle?

Most applications will focus on one of three relationships: with God ... within yourself ... with other people. Think of applying as the palm of your grip on the Bible.

Quick Review

- ➢ The Bible consists of 66 books arranged by type.
- ➢ The writers of the Bible were inspired by God, and the revelation was not based on their own interpretation.
- ➢ The Bible is our highest authority in every area of life.
- ➢ You should get a grip on your Bible by
  - o Hearing
  - o Reading
  - o Studying
  - o Memorizing
  - o Meditating
  - o Applying

Scripture Memory Course

Live the New Life:

Christ the Center	2 Corinthians 5:17; Galatians 2:20
Obedience to Christ	Romans 12:1; John 14:21
The Word	2 Timothy 3:16; Joshua 1:8
Prayer	John 15:7; Philippians 4:6-7
Fellowship	Matthew 18:20; Hebrews 10:24
Witnessing	Matthew 4:19; Romans 1:16

Proclaim Christ

All have sinned	Romans 3:23; Isaiah 53:6
Sin's penalty	Romans 6:23; Hebrews 9:27
Christ paid the penalty	Romans 5:8; 1 Peter 3:18
Salvation not by works	Ephesians 2:8-9; Titus 3:5
Must receive Christ	John 1:12; Revelations 3:20
Assurance of Salvation	1 John 5:13; John 5:24

Rely on God's Resources:

His Spirit	1 Corinthians 3:16; 1 Corinthians 2:12
His Strength	Isaiah 41:10; Philippians 4:13
His Faithfulness	Lamentations 3:22; Numbers 23:19
His Peace	Isaiah 26:3; 1 Peter 5:7
His Provision	Romans 8:32; Philippians 4:19
His Help in Temptation	Hebrews 2:18; Psalms 119:9,11

Be Christ's Disciple:

Put Christ first	Matthew 6:33; Luke 9:23
Separate from the World	1 John 2:15, Romans 12:2
Be steadfast	1 Corinthians 15:58; Hebrews 12:3
Serve others	Mark 10:45; 2 Corinthians 4:5
Give generously	Proverbs 3:9-10; 2 Corinthians 9:6-7
Develop World Vision	Acts 1:8; Matthew 28:19-20

Grow in Christ Likeness:

Love	John 13:34-35; 1 John 3:18
Humility	Philippians 2:3-4; 1 Peter 5:5-6
Purity	Ephesians 5:3; 1 Peter 2:11
Honesty	Leviticus 19:11; Acts 24:16
Faith	Hebrews 11:6; Romans 4:20-21
Good Works	Galatians 6:9-10; Matthew 5:16

Dr. Jeffery Elliott

Prophecy

And we have the word of the prophets made more certain, and you will do well to pay attention to it, ... you must understand that no prophecy of Scripture came about by the prophet's own interpretation. For prophecy never had its origin in the will of man, but men spoke from God as they were carried along by the Holy Spirit. 1 Peter 1:19-21

In this chapter you will learn:

➢ The major world empires outlined in Bible prophecy and which ones have come to pass

➢ How prophecy identifies Jesus as the Messiah

➢ What End Times Prophecy is

➢ Reasons to believe we are living in the End Times

➢ A timeline of End Times events

The study of prophecy is fascinating. It shows how God told us what would happen in great detail. It is one of the most convincing evidence that Jesus is the Messiah. It tells us what we can expect from the return of Jesus Christ. This chapter will only cover a small sample of important prophecies.

Daniel's Visions of the Progression of World Empires

The book of Daniel records the progression of world kingdoms from the Babylonian Empire to the final World Empire of the Antichrist through a series of visions given to King Nebuchadnezzar and Daniel. They have been amazingly accurate. The visions give more and more detail about the empires as they progress from one to the next. Instead of just vague ramblings, the visions give great detail which history has verified and even contains interpretations that identify the world empires. The following table shows these kingdoms with two of the visions. Read the passages to see the detail.

World Kingdoms	Daniel 2:1-45 Statue	Daniel 7:1-28 Four Beasts
Babylonian	Gold Head	Lion
Persian/Medes	Silver Chest	Bear
Grecian	Bronze Belly	Leopard
Roman	Iron Legs	Fourth Beast
Final Human	Iron Mixed with Clay	Fourth Beast
Kingdom of God	Mountain	

The first vision is of a statue made of different materials and the second vision is of four beasts. Daniel 2 introduces the panoramic idea of the rise of these kingdoms throughout the future until the return of Christ and the establishment of the Kingdom of God. The first four empires, the Babylonian through the Roman, have passed. The final empire to rise will be an alliance of ten kings represented by the ten toes. Then the mountain, representing the Kingdom of God, will replace all human governments.

Daniel 7 gives more detail that allows us to identify the different empires. In chapter eight Daniel is given the names of the Persian and Grecian empires (Daniel 8:20-22). The angel that is giving Daniel the interpretation of his vision tells him that the four horns that replace the large horn on the shaggy goat are four kingdoms that arise after the fall of the great king of Greece. That great king was Alexandra the Great who died at the age of 32. His four generals divided his empire among themselves creating the four kingdoms. The general Ptolemy took Egypt. General Seleucas took Syria. Lysimachus took Thrace and Cassander ruled over Macedonia and Greece.

Read Daniel 5 to learn about the transition from the Babylonian Kingdom to the Persian/Medes Kingdom.

Prophecies Identifying Jesus as the Messiah

The Old Testament contains prophecies that act as a fingerprint for the Messiah. Each prophecy helps to narrow down the identity. It is much the same way as sending a letter to one of the six billion people living on this planet. By properly addressing the envelope, you can get a letter to one person in six billion. Your address narrows it down from one country to one street, to one house, apartment, or post office box. Finally, you include the name, and your letter gets to that one person.

For the prophecies from the Old Testament, there is only one person out of all the people that have lived who could have fulfilled all of them. That one person is the Messiah. The Bible says it would be a descendant of Abraham (Gen. 12:3), a descendant of Isaac (Gen 17:19), of the tribe of Judah (Gen. 49:10). Just these identifications of Messiah eliminate billions of people. The prophecies continue to narrow it down. He was to be born in Bethlehem (Micah 5:1-5), a tiny village. He was to be born of a virgin (Isaiah 7:14; Gen. 3:15). Infants would be massacred at his birth (Jer. 31:15). He would be preceded by a forerunner (Malachi 3:1). He would be betrayed by a friend (Psalm 41:9) and sold for 30 pieces of silver (Zach. 11:12-13). But the most amazing prophecy is the prophesied date of the crucifixion of the Messiah found in Daniel 9:24-27. This section of scripture tells us that from the decree from Artaxerxes (Neh. 2:1-8) to rebuild Jerusalem, there would be 483 years till Messiah. This brings us to the date of A.D. 31; the date Jesus was crucified.

End Times Prophecy

The Bible tells us that there will be an end to this world. Jesus will return and will establish a new kingdom that will be an eternal kingdom ruled by Jesus. This present earth will pass away, and a new earth and a new heaven will be created. God will create a great city called New Jerusalem. It will be in New Jerusalem where we will spend eternity with God. Many prophecies in the Bible tell us what the end of the world will be like and what signs will indicate that we are near the end. These are called End Times Prophecies.

Reasons to Believe We are in the End Times

Jesus told us that 'no man knows the day or hour' of his return. But that we should watch for signs of his coming much the same way we watch for signs of a storm coming. Some of the indications that suggest we are in the End Times are the following.

Creation of an Israeli Nation

The creation of the current nation of Israel did not occur until 1948. Since several prophecies deal with the nation of Israel, scholars for centuries tried to find explanations for how these prophecies would be fulfilled without a formal nation of Israel. Since the creation of the nation of Israel, these prophecies can now be fulfilled where they could not have been fulfilled a

98

century ago.

Active movement to rebuild the Temple   Dan 9:26-27

Daniel prophesied that the Antichrist would stop sacrifices in the middle of the 7-year tribulation and would bring about abominations in the temple. The sacrifices can only be made in the temple. Therefore, there must be a temple for this prophecy to be fulfilled. For the last few decades, there has been an active movement among Jews to rebuild the temple. There are three possible locations for the temple to be built according to Jewish scholars. Two of the locations would not require the destruction of the Dome of the Rock. They are getting closer and closer to the rebuilding.

The 2 Witnesses   Rev. 11:3-12

Revelation tells us that there will be two witnesses who will prophesy for 1260 days and then be killed by the Antichrist and lay unburied in the streets of Jerusalem for three and a half days and 'men from every people, tribe, language and nation will gaze on their bodies.' Until just the last few years, it was not possible for such a viewing around the world. With the advent of the internet, viewing the bodies is possible.

One World Government   Daniel 7:23-26

Daniel prophesied that the Antichrist would bring the world together into a final one-world government. This must take place in a relatively short time. A century ago, it would have been impossible for the world to be brought into a one-world government without an extended war taking decades. However, current world conditions and advances in technology make it increasingly easy for a one-world government to be formed in a very short time.

The Mark of the Beast   Rev. 13:16-17

Revelation tells us that during the 7-year tribulation, the Antichrist will require everyone to receive a mark either on their forehead or their right hand. Without this mark, a person would not be allowed to buy or sell. Implementing such a mark and keeping track of it so no one would be able to bypass it would be a nightmare without advanced, fast computers and an electronic purchasing network already in place. With the advent of credit cards and the rapidly advancing computer market, such a scheme would be easy to implement today. At least two electronics companies have developed a small chip that can be injected under the skin of a human that can be scanned and identified. Similar chips are already in use with pets to help identify lost pets. These chips could reasonably be used in place of credit cards and use the existing computer network the credit card company and stores use for purchases. Even tattoos could be used today with the wide use and acceptance they have received.

Timeline of End Times Events

Here is a basic timeline of events from Revelation.

Rapture   Rev. 4:1-2; 1 Thess. 4:13-18

Tribulation

    7 Seals   Rev. 6:1-17; 8:1-2

    7 Trumpets   Rev. :2-9:21; 1:15-19

    7 Bowls   Rev. 15:1-16:21

Glorious Appearing of Christ   Rev. 19:11-21

Battle of Armageddon   Rev. 19:19-21

Millennium (1,000-year reign)   Rev. 20:1-6

New Jerusalem – New Heaven and New Earth   Rev. 21

Quick Review

- ➢ Through Daniel, God gave us a list of the world empires. These were
  - o The Babylon Empire of Nebuchadnezzar
  - o The Persian & Mede Empire of Cyrus
  - o The Grecian Empire of Alexander the Great
  - o The Roman Empire
  - o The final one world government of the Anti-Christ.
- ➢ Of the Empires prophesied, all but the last have come to pass. Once the Empire of the Anti-Christ is passed, the eternal Kingdom of God will be established.
- ➢ There are over 100 unique prophecies identifying Jesus as the Messiah. Some of these prophecies were made 4,000 years before his birth.
- ➢ God has told us there will be an end to this world and that Jesus will return for his followers.
- ➢ Recent world conditions indicate that we are living in the end times.
- ➢ Jesus told us that no one knows the day or the hour but that we are to look for the signs indicating that his return is near.
- ➢ The Bible has also indicated a timeline of end times events.

Scriptures on Prophecies on The Coming of The Messiah

Prophecy	O.T. Ref.	N.T. Fulfillment
Seed of the Woman	Gn 3:15	Gl 4:4, He 2:14
Through Noah's sons	Gn 9:27	Lk 6:36
Seed of Abraham	Gn 12:3	Mt 1:1, Gl 3:8, Gl 3:16
Seed of Isaac	Gn 17:19, 21:12	Ro 9:7, He 11:18
Blessing to nations	Gn 18:18	Gl 3:8
Blessing to Gentiles	Gn 22:18, 26:4	Gl 3:8, Gl 3:16, He 6:14
Blessing through Abraham	Gn 28:14	Gl 3:8, Gl 3:16, He 6:14
Of the tribe of Judah	Gn 49:10	Rv 5:5
No bone broken	Ex 12:46, Num 9:12	Jn 19:36
Blessing to firstborn son	Ex 13:2	Lk 2:23
Serpent in wilderness	Nu 21:8-9	Jn 3:14-15
A star out of Jacob	Nu 24:17-19	Mt 2:2, Lk 1:33,78, Rv 22:16
As a prophet	Dt 18:15, 18:19	Jn 6:14, 7:40, Ac 3:22-23
Cursed on the tree	Dt 21:13	Gl 3:13
The throne of David	2 Sm 7:12,13,16,25,26	Mt 19:28, 21:4, 25:31
established forever	1 Ch 17:11-14, 23-27	Mk 12:37, Lk 1:32, Jn 7:4
	2 Ch 21:7	Ac 2:3, 13:23, Ro 1:3
A promised redeemer	Jb 19:25-27	Jn 5:28-29, Gl 4:4
Declared to be the Son of God	Ps 2:1-12	Mt 3:17, Mk 1:11, Ac 4:25-26
His resurrection	Ps 16:8-10	Ac 2:27, 13:35, 26:23
Hands and feet pierced	Ps 22:1-31	Mt 27:31,35,36
Mocked and insulted		Mt 27:39-43, 45-49
Soldiers case lots for coat		Mk 15:20,24,25,34, Lk 19:24
Accused by false witnesses	Ps 27:12, 35:11	Mt 26:60-61
He commits His spirit	Ps 31:5	Lk 23:46
No bone broken	Ps 34:20	Jn 19:36
Hated without reason	Ps 35:19, 69:4	Jn 15:24-25
Friends stand afar off	Ps 38:1	Mt 27:55, Mk 15:40, Lk 23:49
"I come to do thy will"	Ps 40:6-8	He 10:5-9
Betrayed by a friend	Ps 41:9	Mt 26:14-16, 47, 50
Known for righteousness	Ps 45:2,6,7	He 1:8-9
His resurrection	Ps 49:15	Mk 16:6
Betrayed by a friend	Ps 55:1214	Jn 13:18
His ascension	Ps 68:18	Ep 4:8
Stung by reproaches	Ps 69:9	Jn 2:17, To 15:3
Given gall and vinegar	Ps 69:21	Mt 27:34,48, Mk 15:23
Exalted by God	Ps 72:1-19	Mt 2:2, Php 2:9-11, He 1:8

He speaks in parables	Ps 78:2	Mt 13:34-35
Seed of David exalted	Ps 89:3,4,19,27-29	Lk 1:32, Ac 2:30, 13:23
Son of Man comes in glory	Ps 102:16	Lk 21:24,27, Rv 12:5-10
"Thou remainest"	Ps 102:24-27	He 1:10-12
Prays for His enemies	Ps 109:4	Lk 23:34
Another to succeed Judas	Ps 109:7-8	Ac 1:16-20
A priest like Melchizedek	Ps 110:1-7	Mt 22:41-45, 26:64
The chief corner stone	Ps 118:22,23	Mt 21:42
The King comes in the name of the Lord	Ps 118:26	Mt 21:9, 23:39, Mk 11:9
Declared to be the Son of God	Pr 30:4	Ro 10:6-9, 2 Pe 1:17
Repentance for the nations	Is 2:2-4	Lk 24:47
Hearts are hardened	Is 6:9-10	Mt 13:14-15, Jn 12:39-40
Born of a virgin	Is 7:14	Mt 1:22-23
A rock of offense	Is 8:14-15	Ro 9:33, 1 Pe 2:8
Light out of darkness	Is 9:1-2	Mt 4:14-16, Lk 2:32
God with us	Is 9:6-7	Mt 1:21,23, Lk 1:32-33
Full of wisdom and power	Is 11:1-10	Mt 3:16, Jn 3:34, Ro 15:12
Reigning in mercy	Is 16:4-5	Lk 1:31-33
Nail in a sure place	Is 22:21-25	Rv 3:7
Death swallowed up in victory	Is 25:6-12	1 Co 15:54
A stone in Zion	Is 28:16	Ro 9:33, 1 Pe 2:6
The deaf hear the blind see	Is 29:18-19	Mt 5:3, 11:5, Jn 9:39
King of kings, Lord of lords	Is 32:1-4	Rv 19:16, 20:6
Son of the Highest	Is 33:22	Lk 1:32, 1 Tm 1:17, 6:15
Healing for the needy	Is 35:4-10	Mt 9:30, 11:5, 12:22, 20:34
Prepare ye the way of the Lord	Is 40:3-5	Mt 3:3, Mk 1:3, Lk 3:4-5
The Shepherd dies for Sheep	Is 40:10-11	Jn 10:11, He 13:20
The Meek Servant	Is 42:1-16	Mt 12:17-21, Lk 2:32
A light to the Gentiles	Is 49:6-12	Ac 13:47, 2 Co 6:2
Scourged and spat upon	Is 50:6	Mt 26:67, 27:26-30, Mk 14:65
Rejected by His people	Is 52:13-53:12	Mt 8:17, 27:1,2,12-14,38
Suffered vicariously		Mk 15:3,4,27,28
Silent when accused		Jn 1:29, 11:49-52, 12:37-38
Crucified with transgressors		Ac 8:28-35, 10:43, 13:38-39
Buried with the rich		1 Co 15:3, Ep 1:7
Calling of those "not a people"	Is 55:4-5	Jn 18:37, Ro 9:25-26, Rv 1:5
Deliverer out of Zion	Is 59:16-20	Ro 11:26-27
Nations walk in the Light	Is 60:1-3	Lk 2:32
Anointed to preach liberty	Is 61:1-3	Lk 4:17-19, Ac 10:38

Called by a new name	Is 62:1-2	Lk 2:32, Rv 3:12
Thy King cometh	Is 62:11	Mt 21:5
A vestured dipped in blood	Is 63:1-3	Rv 19:13
Afflicted with the afflicted	Is 63:8-9	Mt 25:34-40
The elect shall inherit	Is 65:9	Ro 11:5,7, He 7:14, Rv 5:5
The Lord our righteousness	Jr 23:5-6	Jn 2:19-21, Ro 1:3-4
Born a King	Jr 30:9	Jn 18:37, Rv 1:5
Massacre of infants	Jr 31:15	Mt 2:17-18
Conceived by the Holy Spirit	Jr 31:22	Mt 1:20, Lk 1:35
A New Covenant	Jr 31:31-34	Mt 26:27-29, Mk 14:22-24
A spiritual house	Jr 33:15-17	Jn 2:19-21, Ep 2:20-21
A tree planted by God	Ezk 17:22-24	Mt 13:31-32
The humble exalted	Ezk 21:26-27	Lk 1:52
The good Shepherd	Ezk 34:23-24	Jn 10:11
Stone cut without hands	Dn 2:34-35	Ac 4:10-12
His Kingdom triumphant	Dn 2:44-45	Lk 1:33, 1 Co 15:24, Rv 11:15
An everlasting dominion	Dn 7:13-14	Mt 24:30, Mk 14:61-62
Kingdom for the saints	Dn 7:27	Lk 1:33, 1 Co 15:24, Rv 11:15
Time of His birth	Dn 9:24-27	Mt 24:15-21, 27:30, Lk 3:1
Israel restored	Ho 3:5	Jn 18:37, Ro 11:25-27
Flight into Egypt	Ho 11:1	Mt 2:15
Promise of the Spirit	Jl 2:28-32	Ac 2:17-21, Ro 10:13
The sun darkened	Am 8:9	Mt 24:29, Ac 2:20, Rv 6:12
Born in Bethlehem	Mi 5:1-5	Mt 2:1, Lk 2:4,10-11
Triumphal entry	Zc 9:9-10	Mt 21:4-5, Mk 11:9-10
Sold for 30 pieces of silver buys Potter's field	Zc 11:12-13	Mt 26:14-15, Mt 27:9
Piercing of his body	Zc 12:10	Jn 19:34,37
Shepherd smitten	Zc 13:1,6,7	Mt 26:31, Jn 16:32
Preceded by forerunner	Ml 3:1	Mt 11:10, Mk 1:2, Lk 7:27
Our sins purged	Ml 3:3	He 1:3

Your New Family

On this rock I will build my church, and the gates of Hades will not overcome it. Matthew 16:18

In this chapter you will learn:

- ➤ The Purpose of the church
- ➤ The Structure of the church
- ➤ The Connections of the church

The Purpose of The Church

Often, we go through the motions of life without ever knowing why we do things we've always done. It is like the newly married husband who was curious why his wife cut off a chunk of the ham before cooking it. He asked her why and her response was, "because Mom always did." Later, while visiting her mother, she asked her why she always cut a portion of the ham off before cooking it. Her mother told her it was because her Mother had always done it. So they asked the Grandmother, and she said because the ham didn't fit in her pan.

We get our first two reasons for existing from the Great Commandment and its compliment found in Matthew 22:34-40:

"Love the Lord your God with all your heart and with all your soul and with all your mind... Love your neighbor as yourself."

Worship

Loving the Lord with all your heart, soul, and mind is worship. Since this is the greatest of all commandments, then it would naturally be one of the purposes of the church.

List some ways you can think of that we worship.

> _____

> _____

> _____

Ministry

Love your neighbor as yourself is ministry.

List some ways you can think of that we do ministry.

> _____

> _____

> _____

We get our next two reasons for existing from the Great Commission found in Matthew 28:19-20

"Therefore go and make disciples of all nations, baptizing them in the name of the Father and of the Son and of the Holy Spirit, and teaching them to obey everything I have commanded you. And

surely I will be with you always, to the very end of the age."

Evangelism

Going and making disciples is the work of evangelism. It is the task of the church to seek to bring others into the kingdom. The word evangel means "Good News" and evangelism is telling the "Good News" about salvation.

List some ways you can think of that we do evangelism.

- ➤ _____
- ➤ _____
- ➤ _____
- ➤ _____

Fellowship

To be baptized into the church is to be brought into the fellowship of the church. To be part of the fellowship means to have a relationship with the other members of the church.

List some ways you can think of that we do fellowship.

- ➤ _____
- ➤ _____
- ➤ _____

Discipleship

"Teaching them to obey everything I have commanded you" is called discipleship. Discipleship helps Christians know God's Word so they can live by its teachings. It is through discipleship that we see the power of God change lives.

List some ways you can think of that we do discipleship.

- ➤ _____

➢ _____

➢ _____

The Structure of The Church

The Scriptures identify two positions of formal leadership in the church; Pastors and Deacons. (Phil. 1:1; 1 Tim. 3:1-13)

Pastoral Staff

The pastoral staff of Baptist churches is made up of paid professional ministers. Most churches only have one pastor. The purpose of the pastoral staff is to guide the church, minister to the membership and administer the ministries of the church. The pastor in a baptist church is usually selected by a committee appointed by the congregation. The requirements for a pastor are listed in 1 Timothy 3:1-7 and are as follows:

➢ Above reproach
➢ Husband of but one wife
➢ Temperate
➢ Self-controlled
➢ Respectable
➢ Hospitable
➢ Able to teach
➢ Not given to much wine
➢ Not violent but gentle
➢ Not quarrelsome
➢ Not a lover of money
➢ Must manage his own family well
➢ His children should show him respect
➢ Not a recent convert
➢ Good reputation with outsiders

Deacons

Deacons first appear in Acts 6:1-7 The Greek term for deacon means servant. The original purpose of the deacons was to serve the members of the church. The qualifications for deacons is found in 1 Timothy 3:8-23 and are:

- ➤ Worthy of respect
- ➤ Sincere
- ➤ Not indulging in much wine
- ➤ Not pursuing dishonest gain
- ➤ Keep hold of the deep truths of the faith
- ➤ Husband of but one wife
- ➤ Manage his children and household well
- ➤ Wives are to be women worthy of respect
  - o Not malicious talkers
  - o Temperate
  - o Trustworthy in everything

Some churches see a third group of formal leadership called elders. In these churches, elders function as spiritual leadership only. However, most Baptist churches see the terms for deacons and elders as interchangeable in the Bible. Paul writes the requirements for a deacon to young Timothy but does not mention elders. Then Paul writes to young Titus and refers only to elders with similar requirements as the deacons of 1Timothy, but he does not mention deacons.

Officers

The officers of the church are volunteers who take on the necessary administration of certain church functions such as financial, legal, and ministry matters. Assistants for each office are also appointed to fill in when the officer is unable to perform his or her duties. The officers are usually recommended by the Church

Council and voted on by the congregation each year. Examples of officers are:

Council and voted on by the congregation each year. Examples of officers are:

- Moderator
- Clerk
- Treasurer
- Trustees
- Song Leader
- Pianist
- Organist
- Nursery Coordinator
- Mission Board Representative
- WMU Director
- Youth Director
- Music Director
- Children's Director
- Sunday School Director

Committees/Teams

Committees or teams are an opportunity for members to serve their church. They are usually groups of three or more people who work together to accomplish a task for the church. Committee members are usually recommended by the Church Council and voted on by the congregation.

Teachers

Sunday School teachers and assistants are recommended by the Church Council and voted on by the congregation each year. They serve in the Sunday School by teaching or leading a class.

The Connections of a Baptist Church

As a local body of Christ, we are very interested in accomplishing what the Lord wants us to do. However, there are things we cannot accomplish on our own. We work with other churches to be able to do more than we can do by ourselves. For Southern Baptist churches there are three levels of cooperation.

Local Association

Baptist churches work with other churches in their local area to be able to provide local ministries and resources that would be difficult for one church to provide on its own. This local cooperation is called an association. Participation in a local association is voluntary. The association has no authority over the participating churches and does not make policy, doctrinal, or administration decisions for the local church.

State Convention

Local churches can also join with churches across the state to provide ministries and resources on a much larger scale. Like the local association, participation in the state convention is voluntary, and the state convention has no authority over the participating churches, nor does it make policy, doctrinal, or administration decisions for these churches.

National Convention

Churches also work across the United States in the National Convention known as the Southern Baptist Convention (SBC). The SBC was organized in 1845 in Augusta Georgia and has 15.9 million members and over 47,272 churches. There are 1,136 local associations and 42 state conventions that work with the SBC. Membership in the SBC is voluntary, and the SBC has no authority or decision-making power over the local church. The national convention can do ministries such as international and North American missions that would not be possible if all the churches simply operated on their own. Through a program known as the Cooperative Program, all SBC churches cooperate by sending a regular percentage of their tithes and offerings to support these ministries. The SBC has the largest missionary organization in the world. There are over 5,000 missionaries in the United States and 3,562 foreign missionaries in 153 nations.

Your Piece of The Puzzle

Now you are the body of Christ, and each one of you is a part of it.
1 Corinthians 12:27

In this chapter you will learn:

- ➤ Why you are a minister

- ➤ How you are gifted for ministry

- ➤ What an ideal church member would look like

Every Member A Minister

When you hear the term "minister" you probably think of a pastor, minister of music or some other paid position. But the Bible has a different use for the term "minister." According to the Bible, every Christian is a minister. You may not preach or lead some ministry, but you serve the Lord with your talents, abilities, and skills. Paul compares the church to the human body. The human body is made up of many parts such as eyes, arms, legs, and so on. Yet, the body is a unit and does not function properly without all of its parts working together. The same is true of the church. It is a unit that is made up of many parts such as preachers, Sunday School teachers, nursery workers, and so on. It is also like a big jigsaw puzzle. If there is a piece missing, the puzzle is incomplete. As a member, you are a piece of the your church's puzzle, and without you we are incomplete.

Gifted For Ministry

You may be questioning just what you can do to serve God and the church. Don't worry. In 1 Corinthians 12, Paul tells us that when you received Christ as your Savior, you also received the Holy Spirit. That means the Holy Spirit lives inside you. And the Holy Spirit has given you a spiritual gift for you to use in the work of the church. So what kinds of gifts are there? The Bible gives us four lists of spiritual gifts. These lists contain different gifts, which means the writers were giving some examples and not a complete list of every spiritual gift. For now, let's look at the four lists.

Romans 12:6-8	1 Corinthians 12:7-10;28-29	Ephesians 4:11	1 Peter 4:10-11
Prophecy	Wisdom	Apostles	Speaking
Serving	Knowledge	Prophecy	Serving
Teaching	Faith	Evangelizing	
Encouraging	Gifts of Healing	Pastoring	
Contributing	Miraculous Powers	Teaching	
Leadership	Prophecy		
Mercy	Discernment		

	Tongues		
	Interpretation of Tongues		
	Apostles		
	Teaching		
	Administration		

Prophecy/Speaking

The gift of prophecy should not be confused with fortune telling. It is the gift of preaching the Word of God. Looking at the prophets of the Old Testament we see that they were the preachers of the day. Although they did foretell of coming events, most of their time was devoted to preaching the Word of God.

Speaking is the gift of public speaking for Christ. Although this includes preaching, it indicates a broader use of the public speaking than what most think of as preaching.

Serving

Serving is the gift of wanting to help in whatever way is needed and is usually a behind-the-scenes gift.

Teaching

God has gifted some to be able to understand and explain the deep truths of scripture. This is the gift of teaching.

Encouraging

The gift of encouraging is demonstrated in someone who sees

the need for encouragement and with a word, a call, or a card can just lift the spirits of another.

Contributing

This gift goes beyond the normal tithe. This gift is demonstrated by someone who looks for financial needs and quietly seeks to fill them.

Leadership

This gift is the ability to lead others.

Mercy

This is the gift of compassionately ministering to those who are hurting.

Wisdom

This is the gift of understanding the deep things of the gospel.

Knowledge

This is the gift of applying the truths of scripture to the real world.

Faith

This is a faith that goes beyond the usual faith. It is an unshakeable belief that God can do whatever he says. It is a great encouragement to the church and leads the church to accomplish great things.

Gifts of Healing

This is a gift of actual healing. It is rare today and can be seen in people who pray for the sick where visible results are seen.

Miraculous Powers

This is the gift of seeing real miracles from your prayers and faith.

Discernment

This is the gift of recognizing false teachings and false teachers.

Tongues

This is the ability to speak in another language. It is usually thought of as the ability to speak in a language you have never studied. However, I believe that today this gift can be seen in those who have a knack for picking up languages easily for the purpose of sharing the Gospel (such as a missionary to a foreign country).

Interpretation of Tongues

This is the ability to interpret a foreign language. It is usually associated with a language you have not studied.

Administration

This is the gift of being able to coordinate and manage.

Apostles

There are several views on this gift, but I believe the most Biblical is that the original Apostles were gifts from God to the church and today we still benefit from that gift through the New Testament.

Evangelizing

This is the gift of seeing great results from your efforts in witnessing and preaching evangelistic messages.

Pastoring

This is the gift of shepherding people. It can be used in more than just the office of pastor of a church. It can be used in any area where you oversee, comfort, guide, and encourage people.

Truths About Spiritual Gifts

➤ Only Christians have them (1 Cor. 2:14)
➤ Every Christian has at least one (1 Cor. 7:7)
➤ No Christian has all the gifts (1 Cor. 12:27-30)
➤ No single gift is given to all Christians (1 Cor. 12:29-30)
➤ The Holy Spirit decides what gift you get (1 Cor. 12:11)
➤ The gifts are not to you but the church (Eph. 4:12)

How to Determine Your Spiritual Gifts

There are several worksheets that can be helpful for finding your spiritual gifts. However, most are geared for people who have been a Christian long enough to have had opportunities to use their gifts already. If you are a new Christian, these worksheets may not be very helpful. The best way to determine your spiritual giftedness is a simple three-step plan.

1. Ask God to show you your spiritual gifts
2. Look for opportunities within the church to serve
3. Evaluate your effectiveness in your service to see if you found your spiritual gift

The Ideal Church Member

The ideal church member both gives and receives. There is a sense of commitment to the church as much as there is to Christ himself. Since Christ gave himself up for the church (Eph. 5:25), He apparently considers the church very important and is greatly committed to the church. We should be just as committed to church as Christ. Here are some ways the ideal church member is committed to his church.

Church Attendance

A Kentucky middle school published the following policy statement:

"The middle school SBDM Council believes there is a direct relationship between regular attendance and academic success. The Middle School Attendance Policy reflects the importance of students being in school."

It does not take a genius to see that if you are not in class, you won't learn the material. I learned this the hard way as a freshman in college. A friend of mine agreed to attend our second quarter calculus class every other day, and I would attend the days he missed. We would share the information we learned and be able to sleep in an hour later every other day. The result was our grade for that quarter dropped an entire letter grade and we were struggling as we entered the third quarter. Obviously, we did not repeat this mistake.

Your attendance in church is vital to your spiritual growth. Satan, your enemy, will try to convince you this is not so. Beware! He is very cunning. He will get you to slip away slowly. At times it will seem like a constant battle to attend church regularly. Don't let him win.

Years ago, *The British Weekly* published this provocative letter:

Dear Sir:

It seems ministers feel their sermons are very important and spend a great deal of time preparing them. I have been attending church quite regularly for thirty years, and I have probably heard 3,000 of them. To my consternation, I discovered I cannot remember a single sermon. I wonder if a minister's time might be more profitably spent on something else?

For weeks a storm of editorial responses ensued … finally ended by this letter:

> Dear Sir:
>
> I have been married for thirty years. During that time I have eaten 32,850 meals – mostly my wife's cooking. Suddenly I have discovered I cannot remember the menu of a single meal. And yet … I have the distinct impression that without them, I would have starved to death long ago.[3]

When you attend church, you receive spiritual blessings that are often overlooked by our carnal side. The importance of these spiritual blessings cannot be overstated. After 20 years of working in the Engineering field, I can say that I never let work keep me from church. Not even Wednesday nights. Even though we lived an hour from my work and a half hour from our church, our family attended Sunday morning, Sunday evening, and Wednesday night. On Wednesday nights, my wife would get the children ready for church and meet me in town at a restaurant for dinner; then we would go on to church. I never regretted the extra time and effort Wednesday nights took.

An elderly deaf man was asked why he attended every service of his church since he could not hear a thing that was going on. He responded, "I just want folks to know whose side I'm on!"

Financially Supporting Your Church

God owns the cattle on a thousand hills (Psalm 50:10), so why does He need your money? God has chosen to support the work of His church through the financial giving of his people. Nowhere in the Bible do we find the early church holding fundraisers. I believe

---

[3] *Fresh Illustrations for Preaching and Teaching : From Leadership Journal.* Baker Books, 1997. Edward K. Rowell editor.

that if every Christian were a tither plus (the plus meaning increasing the percentage as God blesses you with more), then we would have a lot richer Christians and a lot more ministry growing the Kingdom of God. Think about it; if you allow yourself to be a conduit for God's money to flow to God's church for God's kingdom, won't God use that conduit.

Serving Your Church

We've covered this section previously, but the ideal church member would look for a place to serve the church.

Praying for Your Church

The Bible tells us that the "prayer of a righteous man is powerful and effective" (James 5:16). Prayer for your church is very important. This is something that Christians should be doing on a daily basis. Prayer is an effective spiritual weapon (Eph. 6:18). Satan is constantly seeking to destroy the church. One of the ways he uses the most is to bring division and dissension in the church. All the members of the church should be praying daily for the unity of the church (Eph. 4:3). We should also be praying for each other (Eph. 6:18). Pray for the church's evangelism efforts (2 Thess. 3:1).

Your Pastor

A recent study showed that of the most stressful jobs, the job of pastor rates very high. Whatever decision the pastor makes, there is always someone who thinks he should have made a different decision. No matter how he handles a situation, there is someone who thinks it should have been handled differently. Often these people come to the pastor to share their 'concerns.'

Jesus said "strike the shepherd, and the sheep will scatter" (Mark 14:27). Satan will try to attack your pastor to make your church ineffective. Pastors often experience dark times of deep depression, uncertainty, hopelessness, and doubt. Satan will try to use gossip to destroy the ministry and credibility of the pastor. And Satan will always try to lure the pastor into scandal. It is important to support, encourage and pray for your pastor (1 Thess. 5:12-13).

Quick Review

- ➢ You are a minister for Christ
- ➢ God has given you a spiritual gift to be used in the church such as
    - o Prophecy/Speaking
    - o Serving
    - o Teaching
    - o Encouraging
    - o Contributing
    - o Leadership
    - o Mercy
    - o Wisdom
    - o Knowledge
    - o Faith
    - o Gifts of Healing
    - o Miraculous Powers
    - o Discernment
    - o Tongues
    - o Interpretation of Tongues
    - o Administration
    - o Apostles
    - o Evangelizing
    - o Pastoring
- ➢ Truths about spiritual gifts
    - o Only Christians have them (1 Cor. 2:14)
    - o Every Christian has at least one (1 Cor. 7:7)
    - o No Christian has all the gifts (1 Cor. 12:27-30)

- o No single gift is given to all Christians (1 Cor. 12:29-30)
- o The Holy Spirit decides what gift you get (1 Cor. 12:11)
- o The gifts are not to you but the church (Eph. 4:12)
- ➤ How to determine your spiritual gifts
    - o Ask God to show you your spiritual gifts
    - o Look for opportunities within the church to serve
    - o Evaluate your effectiveness in your service to see if you found your spiritual gift
- ➤ An ideal member
    - o Always attends the services of his church
    - o Financially supports his church
    - o Seeks to serve in his church
    - o Prays for his church
    - o Supports, encourages and prays for his pastor

Dictionary of Christian and Religious Words

Amen – a Hebrew word that means "so be it."

Angels – spiritual beings who serve God and do his will. Their tasks include delivering messages from God, serving/ministering to Christians, battling the enemies of God, and worshipping God. The Greek word translated angel means messenger.

Anti-Christ – this term can refer to anything that works against Christ and the Church. Specifically, it refers to a world leader who will unite all nations into one world power (but not necessarily one nation) and will eventually be revered as a god. The peace brought about by this world leader will be short-lived (about 3 and a half years) and will be followed by judgment of mankind by God.

Anti-diluvian – anti means before. Diluvian is derived from deluge, which means flood. Thus, anti-diluvian means before the flood and refers to the period before the flood of Noah.

Apostasy – a falling away. Refers to Christians falling away from the faith.

Apostle – this term carries two meanings. First, it refers to the official title of fourteen men in the new testament identified specifically by Christ. The fourteen were "Simon (who is called Peter) and his brother Andrew; James son of Zebedee, and his brother John; Philip and Bartholomew; Thomas and Matthew the tax collector; James son of Alphaeus, and Thaddaeus; Simon the Zealot and Judas Iscariot" (who betrayed Christ but still was called an Apostle before he betrayed Christ), Mathias (who took Judas' place), and Paul (whom Christ gave the title of Apostle after his conversion). The term means 'one sent' and is sometimes used to mean a missionary or a church planter. Some groups use the term to mean a leader within their ranks who has authority over other leaders and several churches (possibly all the churches within their group).

Born Again – this term comes from the verse found in John 3 where Jesus is speaking to Nicodemus about salvation. It refers to what happens when someone receives Christ. Paul tells us that God creates a new us when we receive Christ. This new us is like a baby, not knowing how to be a Christian but having to learn just like a baby learns. Thus, when we receive Christ, we are 'born again.'

Christian – literally means 'little Christ.' Originally this term was used to ridicule those who followed Christ and tried to live a moral and Godly life. As Christians began using it themselves, the stigmatism was soon forgotten. Today, it means a person who has realized their sinfulness and their inability to get rid of their sins by their actions and have believed on Jesus as their Savior from their sins and have been Born Again (see Born Again).

Christology – A theological term referring to the study of the doctrine of Christ (his deity, nature, etc.).

Communion – a ritual where Christians share in receiving spiritual strength through wine or grape juice as the blood of Christ and bread as the body of Christ. In this ritual, some believe there is a special presence of Christ in the wine/grape juice and bread.

Deacon – a servant in the local church. Often this position carries spiritual leadership.

Demonic - of or having to do with demons.

Demons – angels who rebelled against God with Lucifer. They were cast out of heaven down to earth where they await their final condemnation to the lake of fire (hell). All demons reside on the planet earth, and there are no demons in hell yet. They work under their leader Satan (Lucifer, the Devil, that old Dragon, the Serpent) to thwart the work of God and torture men and women by tempting them to sin and mess up their lives. Their greatest priority is to bring about the domination of the human race by Satan through the Anti-Christ, the Beast, and the False Prophet.

Disciple – literally 'one who follows.' This refers to a person who devotes his life to following a person or a way of living such as a Christian who devotes their life to following Christ and the way he taught us to live.

Ecclesiology – A theological term referring to the study of the doctrine of the church (what it's supposed to do, how it is structured, its development, etc.).

Elder – a spiritual leader who is not a professional priest or pastor. Found both in an Israelite community and a Christian church.

Epistle – a letter.

Eschatology – a theological term referring to the study of the doctrine of End Times (the return of Christ, tribulation, Armageddon, Revelation, Daniel, etc.).

Evangelical – refers to churches or Christians who focus on the work of evangelism (see evangelism). This term has broadened in recent times to include the idea of adhering closely to the morality of the Bible and a literal interpretation of the Bible.

Evangelism / Evangelize – refers to the work of telling people about Christ and salvation to compel them to receive Christ as their Savior.

Fasting – going without food to devote your time and energy to praying, reading and seeking God (or the will of God). There are three types of fasts. A partial fast where you simply give up certain foods for a period (this is also used with non-food items such as TV, sex, sports, etc.). Then there is the normal fast where you give up all food and flavored drinks (anything other than water). This fast is kept under 40 days (health problems can arise after 40 days, but a healthy person can go 40 days without any health problems). Finally, there is the absolute fast where you give up all food and drink (including water). This fast is usually kept under three days (after three days serious health problems can occur including death, which is pretty serious). Up until the last 100 years, fasting was considered a normal regular activity of a Christian.

Glorification – a theological term referring to the change in a Christian's body when Christ comes back. The body changes from a mortal one to an immortal one freed from the curse of sin which brings pain, suffering, and physical needs such as hunger and sleep.

Golgatha – literally 'the place of the skull.' This refers to the place Jesus was crucified.

Gospel – This word has two meanings. The first refers to a unique type of literature found only in the Bible which focuses on the ministry of Christ. Some think of the 'Gospels' as being biographies, but in a literary sense, they are not true biographies. The second meaning of the word refers to the message about Christ and salvation. It comes from the Greek word meaning good news.

Hymn – simply an old religious song usually structured with several different verses and a common chorus. Most hymns in today's hymnals contain less than half of the original verses.

Lord's Supper – a ritual where Christians share in receiving grape juice or wine as a symbol of the blood of Christ and bread as a symbol of the body of Christ. This ritual is done to remember what Christ did on the cross.

Mass – a ritual where Catholics share in receiving grace through drinking wine which they believe has been changed into the actual blood of Christ and eating bread which they believe has been changed into the actual body of Christ.

Pre-millennium – pre means before. Millennium means 1,000 years. Thus, Pre-millennium means before the 1,000-year reign of Christ and is the belief that the rapture will come before the 1,000-year reign of Christ mentioned in Revelation.

Pre-mosaic – pre means before. Mosaic is derived from Moses. Thus, pre-mosaic means before Moses and refers to the period before Moses.

Rapture – what happens to Christians when Christ returns. We are 'caught up' in the air and changed from a mortal body (one that will die) to an immortal body. Those Christians who have already died will be resurrected from the dead with a changed body.

Regeneration – a theological term referring to what happens when we receive Christ. Paul tells us we become a new creation. See Born Again.

Soteriology – A theological term referring to the study of the doctrine of salvation.

Sanctification – a theological term referring to a Christian's spiritual growth after they have received Christ.

Scribe – someone in biblical times who could read and write and who studied the scriptures and gave advice, particularly advice on the Mosaic law. Some put them into the category of lawyers.

Testament – a covenant or agreement between two people or between man and God.

Theology – the study of God. Theo is Latin for God and ology is Latin for study.

Tithe – literally means a tenth. Refers to giving a tenth of your income to the Lord. The idea is that God owns everything and gives you everything you get. Giving a tenth (or tithe) back to God shows that you recognize God as the actual owner.

Zion – another name for Jerusalem. For Christians, it symbolizes the New Jerusalem (heaven).

Kick-Start Your Spiritual Growth
Church Edition

Get a Kick-Start in a custom version for
your church! Begin a Kick-Start class for
new believers or give a copy to your new
believers and let them fast-track their
spiritual growth!

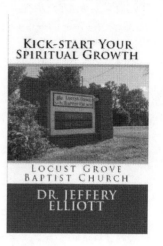

- **Front Cover Customization**
- **Back Cover Customized Pastor's Info**
- **Custom Interior Church Pages**

Visit kick-start-church.com to schedule a consultation

The Story of Kick-Start Your Spiritual Growth Book

As a high school student leading unchurched youth to Christ, I saw them
struggle as I tried to get them integrated into our church's Sunday
School. Much of the teaching and discussion expected a certain amount
of biblical knowledge. Even as the Sunday School teacher tried to "dumb
down" the lesson for the new kids, most of the class grew up in the
church and had an advantage over the new believers. During the
sermons I saw puzzled faces as they struggled with unfamiliar concepts.
It was in that struggle that I realized the need for a fast-paced study that
would bring a new believer "up-to-speed." Four decades later, that
vision is available to you for use in your own ministry setting customized
for your church.

After years of trying a variety of new believer classes in churches where
I was pastor, I decided to design my own class. I chose eleven topics
selected to build a foundation in three areas of a new believer's life:
Their daily walk with Christ, their knowledge and study of the Bible, the
church and their relationship to it.

ABOUT THE AUTHOR

Dr. Jeffery Elliott was born and raised in Clarksville Tennessee. At the age of seven, Dr. Elliott was born again at Hilldale Baptist Church. For over half a century, he has served in churches as a layman, a deacon, and a minister. He has been married to his college sweetheart for almost four decades. In all that they do they have served the Lord together.

Dr. Elliott received his Bachelor of Science in Electrical Engineering from Tennessee Technological University and worked in the field of electrical engineering and computer science for almost 20 years. During that time God called him into bi-vocational ministry and eventually into full-time ministry. In preparation for the ministry, he received a Masters of Divinity degree from Golden Gate Baptist Theological Seminary and a Doctorate of Ministry degree from The Southern Baptist Theological Seminary.

Made in the USA
Columbia, SC
23 May 2022

60827356R00078